Serve up a top grade with CGP!

Struggling with sauces? Confused between calcium and carbs?
Fear not, this CGP revision guide is here to help...

It contains everything you need to know for the AQA exam,
from basic cooking methods to the "hang on, isn't this science?" parts
— plus plenty of questions to test how well you're digesting it all.

At the back, you'll find well-seasoned advice pages for the exam
and non-exam assessments, and a super-handy glossary for garnish.

CGP — still the best! ☺

Our sole aim here at CGP is to produce the highest quality books —
carefully written, immaculately presented and dangerously close to being funny.

Then we work our socks off to get them out to you
— at the cheapest possible prices.

Contents

Section One — Food, Nutrition and Health

Section Two — Food Science

Section Three — Food Safety

Section Four — Food Choice

Section Five — Food Provenance

Section Six — Food Preparation Skills

Published by CGP

Editors:
Liam Dyer, Rob Harrison, Simon Little, Sean Walsh.

Contributors:
Angela Nugent

Proofreaders:
Susan Alexander, Mike Lewis and Glenn Rogers

With thanks to Lesley Woods for the reviewing.

With thanks to Ana Pungartnik for the copyright research.

Photo on p 4 Science Photo Library and p 23 Mark Sykes/Science Photo Library

Photo on p 2 KMI Images / Alamy Stock Photo, p 24 Food and Drink Photos / Alamy Stock Photo,
p 25 funkyfood London ~ Paul Williams / Alamy Stock Photo, p 29 Dale O'Dell / Alamy Stock Photo,
p 30 Westend61 GmbH / Alamy Stock Photo and Myrleen Pearson / Alamy Stock Photo.

ISBN: 978 1 78294 649 6

Printed by Elanders Ltd, Newcastle upon Tyne.
Clipart from Corel®

Based on the classic CGP style created by Richard Parsons.

Proteins

Proteins, fats and carbohydrates are macronutrients. 'Macro' means large, and funnily enough our bodies need these macronutrients in large amounts. First up we have proteins — don't say we never treat you...

Protein is Needed for Growth, Repair and Maintenance

1) We get protein from a wide range of foods, including: meat, fish, dairy products, nuts, seeds and beans.

2) Proteins are made up of amino acids — these can be thought of as the building blocks of the body.

3) Our bodies can make some amino acids (these are called non-essential amino acids) but not others — we have to eat the amino acids our bodies can't make (the essential amino acids).

4) Our bodies need proteins for a variety of reasons:

- Growth — e.g. from childhood to adulthood, and for the growth of nails, hair and muscle mass.
- Repair — e.g. repairing our muscles, tissues and organs after illness or injury.
- Maintenance — e.g. to make enzymes for digestion and antibodies to stop us getting ill.

Proteins Have Different Biological Values

- High biological value (HBV) proteins contain all of the essential amino acids we need.
- They're mainly found in animal sources — e.g. meat, fish, poultry, eggs, cheese and milk.
- Soya beans and quinoa are plant-based HBV protein foods (see next page).

- Low biological value (LBV) proteins are missing one or more of the essential amino acids we need.
- They're only found in plant sources — e.g. peas, lentils, nuts, seeds and most beans, and in smaller amounts in vegetables like spinach and broccoli.

Protein Complementation Combines LBV Protein Foods

1) If we don't get enough HBV protein, we have to combine different LBV proteins to get all the essential amino acids in our diet — this is called protein complementation.

2) For example, hummus and pitta are LBV protein foods (they're missing some essential amino acids), but when we combine the two, the meal as a whole provides all the essential amino acids we need.

With compliments of the chef...

3) If you're eating a balanced diet, you probably combine proteins without realising it — e.g. a vegetable lasagne with six different veggies in the recipe is good protein complementation.

Different People Need Different Amounts of Protein

1) Dietary reference values are estimates of the amount of nutrients people should have in their diet.

2) An average male should consume 55 g and an average female should consume 45 g of protein each day.

3) In reality, the amount of protein different people need varies:

- Growing children need a greater amount of protein relative to their size and body mass.
- Physically active people need more protein for muscle growth and repair.
- Pregnant women need about 6 g more protein than normal to help the baby grow. During breastfeeding, women require even more.

Proteins

I won't pro-tend this stuff is particularly exciting, but proteins are very important to our health...

Too Much or Too Little Protein Causes Problems

An excess (too much) or deficiency (too little) of protein in the diet can have serious consequences:

Excess

- The liver and the kidneys help process proteins. Too much protein in the diet puts a lot of pressure and strain on these organs, which can be dangerous.

Deficiency

- Without protein, growth is slowed down, especially in children who are still growing.
- Because hair, skin and nails don't grow as fast, they can get into a poor condition.
- The immune system can't work properly without protein — this means wounds don't heal as quickly and people have a higher risk of catching infections.
- People struggle to digest food properly, which means some nutrients aren't taken in by the body.
- Protein deficiency can also lead to oedema — a build up of fluid in the body that causes swelling (often around the feet).
- In severe cases, a disease called kwashiorkor can develop. A symptom of the disease is oedema around the stomach, which is why some severely malnourished children have swollen abdomens.

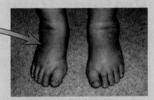

There Are Now Loads of Alternative Proteins

1) Vegetarians don't eat meat, so they need to get their protein from elsewhere.

2) Beans, lentils and nuts are all good sources of protein, as are eggs. There are also alternative proteins:

Soya
- Soya beans are one of the few plant-based HBV protein sources.
- They can be eaten whole (but must be cooked to remove toxicity) in salads, used to make soya milk and processed to make other protein alternatives like tofu and TVP...

Mycoprotein
- Traditionally made from a mushroom-like fungus and egg white (although there are now vegan alternatives that use potato-starch instead).
- It's often used where you'd normally use chicken, and is available as chunks (e.g. for stir-fries), mince (e.g. for chilli con carne) or fillets (e.g. to serve in sauces).

TVP
- TVP (Textured Vegetable Protein) is also made from soya beans — specifically soya flour (made by grinding soya beans).
- The soya flour is used to make a dough which when baked has a meat-like texture and can be made into sausages, burgers and ready meals.

Tofu
- Tofu is made by curdling soya milk.
- It can have different textures depending on how much water it contains: it can be soft (for use in desserts and dips), firm (for use in stir-fries) and extra firm (this is sometimes called dry tofu because it has the least amount of water content).

3) Alternative proteins usually don't taste of much on their own. Luckily, they're great at absorbing the flavours of the foods they're cooked in, e.g. sauces and marinades. There's also a massive range of pre-prepared flavoured alternatives, e.g. bacon-style slices, meat-free chicken fillets, etc.

That youth's no amateur... he's a pro-teen...

Remember the functions of proteins using 'Really Good Macronutrient' (RGM) — repair, growth and maintenance.

Q1   Explain the difference between low biological value proteins and high biological value proteins. [2 marks]

Fats

While it's easy to assume fats are really unhealthy, they're actually an essential part of our daily diet. And just when I was starting to feel guilty about my tower-high stack of chocolate fudge cake...

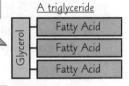

Fats Provide Energy, Nutrients and Insulation

Our bodies need fats for a variety of reasons:

- They provide a concentrated source of energy (twice as much energy per gram as proteins and carbs).
- They are a source of fat-soluble vitamins A, D, E and K (see p.7).
- Fat forms an insulating layer under our skin which keeps us warm.
- These layers of fat also protect our bones and organs (e.g. our heart and kidneys).
- Our bodies also use fat to make cholesterol, which is an essential part of all cell membranes.

Fats Contain Saturated and Unsaturated Fatty Acids

A triglyceride

Glycerol	Fatty Acid
	Fatty Acid
	Fatty Acid

1) Fats are made up of fatty acids and glycerol in the form of triglycerides.
2) Fatty acid chains are made of carbon and hydrogen. They can be saturated or unsaturated — the difference is in how carbon atoms bond with hydrogen atoms:

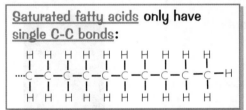

Saturated fatty acids only have single C-C bonds:

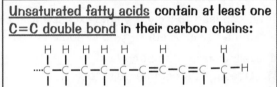

Unsaturated fatty acids contain at least one C=C double bond in their carbon chains:

3) Our body breaks fat down into fatty acids during digestion — the ratio of saturated to unsaturated fatty acids decides whether it's a saturated or unsaturated fat.

Saturated Fats Are Bad For Your Health...

1) Saturated fats are classed as unhealthy fats, especially if eaten in large amounts.
2) They're generally solid at room temperature and tend to come from animal sources such as meats (including processed meats like sausages and burgers), butter, lard, suet and cheese, but they can also come from plant sources like coconut butter.
3) Too much saturated fat in the diet can increase cholesterol levels in the blood, which can increase the risk of coronary heart disease (see next page).

... Unsaturated Fats Are Generally Healthier

1) Unsaturated fats are usually healthier than saturated fats.
2) They're generally soft or liquid at room temperature and come from vegetable sources that are high in fat (e.g. flax seeds and peanuts) and vegetable oils (e.g. sunflower, rapeseed and olive oils).
3) Unsaturated fats can be monounsaturated and polyunsaturated:

- Monounsaturated fats contain one C=C double bond in their carbon chains.
- They are found in foods such as olive oil, almonds, peanut butter and avocados.

- Polyunsaturated fats contain more than one C=C double bond.
- They are found in foods such as sesame oil, soybean oil, seeds and oily fish.

4) Replacing the saturated fats in your diet with unsaturated fats has been shown to lower blood cholesterol — this is why unsaturated fats are often referred to as 'good' fats.

Fats

Without enough fat in our diet, our bodies wouldn't be able to function properly. However, before we get carried away and start bathing ourselves in butter, too much fat can lead to some very serious health problems...

Fats Should Make Up Less Than 35% of Our Daily Food Energy

- According to government guidelines, fat should make up no more than 35% of our food energy per day (see p.16), with no more than 11% of this coming from saturated fat.
- It's recommended that an average adult consume 70 g of fat every day, with a maximum of 20 g of this being saturated fat.
- However, most people in the UK eat more fat than is recommended.

As with protein, the amount of fat a person needs may change depending on age and physical activity.

We Need the Right Amount of Fat in Our Diet

We need to be careful that we have enough but not too much fat in our diet.
A fat excess (too much fat) or fat deficiency (too little fat) can be unhealthy and dangerous:

Excess

- Too much fat can lead to weight gain. Excess fat is stored under the skin and around our organs in some cases.
- Excessive levels of fat in the body lead to obesity (see p.14). Obesity is a common disorder in developed countries such as the UK.
- Obesity can lead to diet-related health issues like type-2 diabetes (see p.15), where the body struggles to control blood sugar levels.
- Too much saturated fat in the diet can increase blood cholesterol levels. Cholesterol builds up in blood vessels such as arteries and restricts blood flow around the body — this increases the risk of high blood pressure, a stroke, a heart attack and coronary heart disease (see p.14).

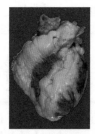

Excess fat in the diet can lead to the build-up of fat around vital organs like the heart (yellow fat can be seen around the red heart muscle).

Deficiency

- A lack of fat in the diet means that less fat-soluble vitamins A, D, E and K are absorbed by the body. This causes vitamin deficiency which leads to various health issues (see p.7).
- If there's also a lack of carbohydrate in the diet, the body will start to use its fat store for energy. Therefore, not eating enough fat can lead to weight loss if there's also a lack of carbohydrate in the diet.
- Less fat means there's less insulation to keep the body warm, and so a person with a fat deficiency will become colder faster.
- It also means there will be a thinner layer of fat under the skin to protect the body from knocks.

Give up my weekly barn dancing class? Fat chance!

It's important you know the differences between saturated and unsaturated fats. A really simple way to get them stuck in your head is to draw out a quick table of all the differences — it's guaranteed to get any party started...

Q1 Give two foods that are high in saturated fat. [2 marks]

Q2 Describe two problems that are associated with a fat deficiency in the diet. [2 marks]

Carbohydrates

Carbohydrates are the final macronutrient we have to look at, whoopee. Get your teeth into this stuff...

Carbohydrates are Needed for Energy

Carbohydrates can be split into two main types: sugar and starch:

- Sugar, e.g. glucose and fructose, can be found in food naturally (e.g. sugars in fruits and vegetables), or can be added to food during the manufacturing process (e.g. sugars in cakes, sweets and fizzy pop).
- Added sugars are often referred to as 'empty calories' because they have no nutritional benefit other than energy.

- Starch can be found in foods such as potatoes, bread, pasta, rice and cereals, as well as vegetables and fruit (in smaller amounts).
- Starchy foods contain lots of nutrients including B vitamins, iron and calcium.
- Wholegrain starch foods also have really high fibre content (see p.64).

When we eat carbohydrate-based foods, our body breaks down the sugar and starch into glucose, which is absorbed into our blood and used by our body for energy.

Simple Carbohydrates are Digested Quickly...

Simple carbohydrates such as sugar can be divided into monosaccharides and disaccharides:

Monosaccharides are the most basic sugar molecules, e.g. glucose and fructose.

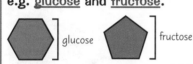

glucose   fructose

Disaccharides are made up of two monosaccharides, e.g. sucrose is made up of glucose and fructose.

sucrose

'Sugary' foods like cakes, jams and sweets are mainly made up of simple carbohydrates.

The body rapidly digests simple carbohydrates, making blood sugar levels rise quickly and providing a short burst of energy.

...While Complex Ones Take Longer to Digest

Complex carbohydrates include 'starchy' foods like wholewheat bread and potatoes.

Complex carbohydrates such as starch are polysaccharides:

Polysaccharides are made up of lots of monosaccharides joined together, e.g. starches are made up of lots of glucose molecules.

...   starch

Complex carbohydrates take a lot longer to digest than simple ones, so they gradually increase blood sugar levels and provide a slow, steady release of energy.

The Glycaemic Index Shows How Carbs Affect Blood Sugar Levels

The glycaemic index (GI) rates carbohydrates on how quickly they affect blood sugar levels:

- High GI foods are digested quickly and cause a rapid rise in blood sugar levels — high GI foods include white bread/pasta/rice, cornflakes and watermelon.
- Low GI foods are digested slowly and cause a gradual rise in blood sugar levels — low GI foods include wholewheat bread/pasta, brown rice, peaches and porridge.

The glycaemic index is especially helpful to people with diabetes because it allows them to choose low GI carbohydrates so they can avoid surges in blood sugar levels.

Carbohydrates

I don't know about you, but I'm in the mood for another page all about <u>carbohydrates</u> — no, just me?...

50% of Our Energy Should Come from Carbs

According to government guidelines, <u>carbohydrates</u> should make up approximately <u>half</u> of our <u>food energy</u> per day (see p.16).

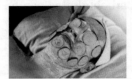

Unfortunately, cucumber face masks don't count towards daily food energy.

- Ideally, <u>most of this energy</u> should come from <u>starchy foods</u> and <u>natural sugars</u> such as those found in bread, pasta, fruit and veg.
- <u>Free sugars</u>, such as those added to food and drinks during manufacturing and those found in sweet foods like syrups and fruit juice, should take up <u>no more than 5%</u>.

On average, people in the UK consume <u>too much sugar</u>. To help with this, food labelling not only has a section for <u>total carbohydrates</u>, but it also has an extra section called <u>'of which sugars'</u> — this helps people separate their sugar intake from their total carb intake (see p.47).

Eating Too Many or Too Few Carbohydrates Is Unhealthy

Like with fat and protein, <u>too much</u> (excess) or <u>too little</u> (deficiency) carbohydrate in our diet is <u>unhealthy</u> and can have <u>serious effects</u> on how our body functions:

Excess

- If we take in more energy from carbohydrates than our body uses, the extra <u>carbohydrate</u> is <u>converted</u> into <u>fat</u>. Too much fat causes <u>obesity</u> and other diet-related health issues (see p.14-15).
- <u>Sugars</u> are the worst for this because they're digested quickly, meaning the <u>energy</u> they provide is ready to use <u>almost immediately</u> — if it's not used quickly, we store it as <u>fat</u>.
- Eating <u>too many sugary foods</u> can lead to <u>tooth decay</u>, sometimes called <u>dental caries</u> (see p.15). <u>Free sugars</u> are the worst type of sugar for tooth decay — e.g. mango juice is more likely to cause tooth decay than if you ate chunks of mango because the sugars are already released and ready to attack your teeth.
- Because <u>simple carbohydrates</u> (e.g. sugar) are <u>quickly digested</u>, they cause <u>rapid surges in blood sugar levels</u> (see previous page). If our blood sugar levels <u>fluctuate</u> (move up and down) too <u>wildly</u> it can lead to the development of <u>type 2 diabetes</u> (see p.15).

The <u>natural sugars</u> in whole fruits are much better for our teeth than the <u>free sugars</u> found in fruit juices.

Deficiency

- A lack of carbohydrate in our diet causes our <u>blood sugar level</u> to <u>drop</u>. This drop can cause <u>hunger</u>, <u>dizziness</u> and <u>tiredness</u> because our body has <u>less energy</u> than it needs.
- If our bodies don't have enough carbohydrate for energy, they need to find another source of energy and will start to use up <u>fat</u> in the diet or body.
- If we also have a fat deficiency then our bodies start to use up <u>protein</u> — this causes us to <u>lose muscle</u>, which makes us <u>weaker</u>.

My parrot loves starch — she's called Polly Saccharide...

That's it for macronutrients. As the name suggests, they're a large part of our nutrition and you need to know the role each of them plays in our diet. They'll show up again later, so it's best to learn them now.

Q1 Name the type of carbohydrate that releases its energy slowly. [1 mark]

Q2 Name one diet-related health problem associated with too much carbohydrate in the diet. [1 mark]

Vitamins — Fat-Soluble

Vitamins, minerals and trace elements are all micronutrients — we need them in small amounts. Vitamins are organic compounds (they come from plants and animals) and are used in processes that keep us alive and well.

Vitamins A, D, E and K are Fat-Soluble

1) Fat-soluble vitamins are found in fatty foods (e.g. meat, fish, animal-based products and vegetable oils).

2) There are four fat-soluble vitamins you need to know about — meet vitamins A, D, E and K:

Vitamin A
- Vitamin A is needed for good eyesight (especially night vision), growth, a healthy immune system and skin — it's also an antioxidant (see next page).
- The main source is retinol, which is found in liver, butter, oily fish and eggs, but it can also be made from carotene (found in margarine and orange or yellow fruit and veg).
+ Too much over time can weaken bones, and foods containing very high levels (e.g. liver) should be avoided during pregnancy.
- Too little can lead to night blindness, a weaker immune system and stunted growth.
- The NHS recommends 0.7 mg of vitamin A for men and 0.6 mg for women each day.

Vitamin D
- Vitamin D helps the body absorb various minerals, including calcium, which is important for the development of healthy bones and teeth.
- It's found in oily fish and egg yolks and is also produced when skin is exposed to sunlight.
+ Too much vitamin D makes you absorb too much calcium — this can lead to kidney damage.
- Too little can lead to bone diseases like osteomalacia (where bones become soft), rickets and osteoporosis (where bones become brittle, see p.15).
- The NHS recommends 0.01 mg of vitamin D a day, although in summer most of us should be able to get enough through natural exposure to the sun.

Vitamin E
- Vitamin E is important because it keeps skin and eyes healthy as well as improving our immune system — as an antioxidant it may protect us from free radicals (see next page).
- It's found in leafy greens (e.g. spinach and kale), broccoli, nuts, vegetable oils and wheat germ.
+ Too much can interfere with blood clotting, cause nausea and blurred vision.
- Too little is rare but leads to weak muscles and problems with sight.
- The NHS recommends 4 mg of vitamin E for men and 3 mg for women each day.

Vitamin K
- Vitamin K helps clot blood, heal wounds and maintain our immune system and bones.
- It's found in leafy greens, cereals and vegetable oils, plus some meats and dairy foods.
+ There is no 'excessive' level of vitamin K.
- Having too little is extremely rare in adults, but it can cause uncontrolled bleeding in newborns.
- The NHS recommends a daily intake 0.001 mg of vitamin K for every kg of body weight.

3) Any fat-soluble vitamins that aren't used up by the body are stored in fat tissue for future use. This means that we don't necessarily need to take in the same amount of each vitamin every day.

4) However, we need to be careful that we don't build up an excess of these vitamins. This is unlikely to occur through a balanced diet — the main risk comes through multivitamin supplements (see p.66).

I'm afraid this isn't a licence to eat cake every day...

Way before we knew about vitamins, the ancient Egyptians would use liver as a treatment for night blindness. These days we know why this remedy was so successful — because of the high level of fat-soluble vitamin A.

Q1   Describe the role vitamin K plays in the body.   [2 marks]

Vitamins — Water-Soluble

Water-soluble vitamins aren't generally stored in the body like fat-soluble ones, so we need to take them in daily.

B Vitamins and Vitamin C are Water-Soluble

'Water-soluble' vitamins dissolve in water — there are lots of them, but you need to know these for the exam:

Vitamin	Function	Sources include	Problems caused by having too little
B1 Thiamin	Helps the nervous system and with energy release from foods.	Bread, pasta, rice, peas, eggs and liver.	Tiredness, weak muscles and beriberi (in severe cases) — a disease that affects the heart, blood vessels and nervous system.
B2 Riboflavin	Helps with energy release from foods and repair of tissues.	Milk, eggs, cheese, and leafy greens.	Dry skin, a sore throat and sores around the mouth.
B3 Niacin	Helps with energy release from foods and maintaining a healthy nervous system and skin.	Wheat, nuts, meat and fish.	Pellagra (a disease causing fatigue, depression and loss of memory).
B9 Folic Acid (or folate)	Crucial for growth, healthy babies and works with vitamin B12 to make red blood cells.	Liver, peas and leafy greens	Anaemia, tiredness, weak muscles and mouth sores. Folic acid is especially important for women planning pregnancy as low levels at conception can cause spina bifida in babies (see p.13).
B12 Cobalamin	Helps the nervous system and works with vitamin B9 to make red blood cells.	Milk, eggs, meat and fish.	Tiredness and nerve damage in extreme cases. Vegans (who don't eat any animal produce) are most likely to have too little.
C Ascorbic acid	Protects the body from infection and allergies, keeps blood vessels healthy and heals wounds.	Citrus fruits, tomatoes, strawberries, green veg and potatoes	Anaemia (see p.14) and scurvy (tiredness and bleeding gums). As vitamin C is an antioxidant, too little can increase the risk of cancer (see below).

Water-soluble vitamins are lost in urine, so in most cases it's unlikely they'll build up to levels where there are serious side effects. However, excessive amounts of vitamin C can cause stomach pain and diarrhoea.

> Arr, I've got a scurvy cutlass.

Prepare Fruit and Veg Carefully to Keep Vitamins

1) Once exposed to air, fruits and veg start losing vitamin C, so prepare them just before you need them.
2) Don't leave your fruits and veg to stand in water because vitamins B and C dissolve into the water. Steaming or microwaving are the best ways to keep these water-soluble vitamins.
3) Don't chop fruit and veg into small pieces as it exposes more of the surface to air and water.

Antioxidants Protect Us from Free Radicals

1) Free radicals are chemicals that we encounter every day of our lives.
2) They're able to damage our body's cells, leading to diseases like cancer and heart disease.
3) Antioxidants (e.g. vitamins A, C and E) are found in foods such as fruit and vegetables — many people believe they help protect our bodies from these damaging free radicals.

Vitamin B Group? — my dad's got one of their records...

There are lots of vitamins to remember on these pages — and yes, you need to know what they do, where they're found and the effects of getting too little (or too much). It might be helpful to write up a Post-it for each vitamin.

Q1   Give one type of food you would recommend to a person suffering from scurvy.   [1 mark]

Minerals and Trace Elements

We also need small amounts of <u>minerals</u> and <u>trace elements</u> in our diet — this nutrition lark is full of surprises...

Calcium, Iron, Sodium and Phosphorus are Minerals

<u>Minerals</u> are chemical elements that our bodies need in small amounts. They help in various <u>chemical reactions</u> in our body and are needed for a variety of reasons:

Calcium
- Calcium is needed for strong <u>bones</u> and <u>teeth</u>, healthy <u>nerves</u> and <u>muscles</u> and blood clotting — <u>growing children</u> need calcium every day to help build strong bones and teeth (see p.12).
- It's found in <u>milk</u>, <u>cheese</u>, <u>tofu</u>, <u>green leafy vegetables</u>, <u>hard water</u> and <u>sesame seeds</u>.
+ <u>Too much</u> calcium is rare, but any excess is stored in organs like the kidneys — this can increase the risk of <u>kidney stones</u> and could even stop the kidneys working.
- <u>Too little</u> calcium during childhood can lead to problems such as <u>rickets</u> and <u>osteoporosis</u> (see p.15) because bones become weaker. It can also slow down blood clotting.

Iron
- Iron is needed to form part of the <u>haemoglobin</u> which gives <u>blood cells</u> their red colour.
- It's found in <u>dark green vegetables</u> (e.g. <u>spinach</u>) and <u>meat</u> (especially <u>liver</u> and <u>kidney</u>).
+ <u>Too much</u> iron is <u>toxic</u> (poisonous) and can cause stomach pains, nausea and constipation. In extreme cases it can even cause death.
- <u>Too little</u> iron causes a deficiency disease called <u>anaemia</u> (see p.14).

Sodium
- Sodium chloride (salt) controls the body's <u>water content</u> and helps our nerves and muscles to function.
- It's found in <u>most foods</u> — many people <u>add</u> it to food as well.
+ <u>Too much</u> salt is <u>bad</u> for you — it can lead to <u>high blood pressure</u> and <u>heart disease</u>. Most people in the UK eat too much salt in their diet.
- <u>Too little</u> salt can cause nausea and muscle cramps.

Phosphorus
- Phosphorus is needed for <u>healthy bones</u> and <u>teeth</u>.
- It's found in <u>protein-rich foods</u> like <u>meat</u>, <u>fish</u>, <u>dairy products</u>, <u>nuts</u>, <u>beans</u> and <u>cereals</u>.
+ <u>Too much</u> phosphorus can make it harder to absorb calcium.
- <u>Too little</u> phosphorus can lead to <u>weak muscles</u> and <u>painful bones</u>.

Fluoride and Iodine are Trace Elements

<u>Trace elements</u> are minerals, but we need them in even <u>smaller amounts</u>:

Fluoride
- Fluoride <u>strengthens teeth</u>, <u>hardens tooth enamel</u> and helps <u>prevent tooth decay</u> (see p.15). The NHS recommends <u>brushing</u> your teeth <u>twice a day</u> with fluoride toothpaste.
- It's found in <u>fish</u>, <u>tea</u>, <u>fluoridated water</u> and <u>dental products</u> (toothpaste and mouthwash).
+ <u>Too much</u> fluoride is <u>toxic</u> and can lead to brown-coloured teeth, bone problems and cancer.
- <u>Too little</u> fluoride can lead to weak teeth and enamel, which leads to <u>tooth decay</u>.

Iodine
- Iodine is needed to make some hormones used by the body.
- It's found in <u>seafood</u>, <u>dairy foods</u> and <u>vegetables</u>.
- A serious lack of iodine can cause <u>goitre</u> (neck swelling) and complications in unborn babies.

In addition to food, <u>minerals</u> and <u>trace elements</u> can be taken in through <u>multivitamin supplements</u> (p.66).

If there's one thing all divers hate, it's hard water...

Remember, we only need a 'trace' of trace elements — because this is such a small amount they're <u>micronutrients</u>.

Q1   Explain the importance of fluoride in our toothpaste.   [2 marks]

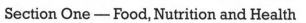

Fibre and Water

As well as proteins, carbs, fats, vitamins, minerals and trace elements we also need <u>fibre</u> and <u>water</u> — blimey!

Fibre Isn't Digested by the Body

Fibre also makes us feel fuller for longer.

1) <u>Fibre</u>, sometimes called <u>NSP</u> (non-starch polysaccharide) or '<u>roughage</u>', is a type of <u>carbohydrate</u> that helps to keep your digestive system <u>working properly</u> and keeps food <u>moving</u> through it. Fibre is found in things like:

    - <u>Vegetables</u> — e.g. peas, beans, broccoli, carrots and potatoes (especially the skin).
    - <u>Fruit</u> and <u>fruit juice</u> — raspberries, prunes, bananas, apples.
    - <u>Brown bread</u> and <u>wholemeal</u> or <u>whole grain</u> foods — e.g. wholemeal bread/rice/pasta/flour.
    - <u>Lentils</u>, <u>beans</u>, <u>seeds</u> and <u>nuts</u>.

2) You need to eat lots of fibre to stay <u>healthy</u>. If you don't, it can lead to <u>health problems</u> such as: <u>constipation</u>, <u>bowel</u> and <u>colon cancer</u>, <u>heart disease</u>, <u>high blood pressure</u>.

3) The NHS states that the average adult should take in <u>30 g</u> of fibre every day. <u>Young children</u> need <u>less fibre</u> because the 'fullness' fibre gives people can stop them from eating foods that contain other important nutrients.

Most people in the UK don't eat enough fibre — some of the health problems mentioned are very common in people over 40.

You Can't Live Without Water

1) Around <u>60%</u> of your body is <u>water</u> — it's found in every cell of your body, as well as fluids like blood, sweat and saliva.

2) Our bodies need water to:

    - <u>Eliminate waste</u> from the body (e.g. excretion)
    - <u>Control body temperature</u> (e.g. sweating)
    - Aid the process of <u>digestion</u>

Steve could always be found loitering by the local watering hole.

3) You get water from <u>drinks</u> like water (obviously), fruit juice, tea, lemonade, etc. It's also found in <u>food</u> — vegetables and fruit contain quite a lot, and even things like meat and bread contain water.

4) Our body loses water in a variety of ways including our sweat, breath, urine and faeces. If you don't drink enough to replace the water you've used or lost, you become <u>dehydrated</u> and your body can't <u>work properly</u>. Dehydration also causes:

    - <u>Slower reactions</u> and <u>poor decision-making</u>, as your <u>brain</u> needs water to function well.
    - <u>Blood to thicken</u>, making it <u>harder</u> for the <u>heart</u> to pump the blood around the body.
    - An <u>increase</u> in <u>body temperature</u> (the body can't sweat effectively).

5) You should have about <u>2 litres</u> of water a day — but if you're <u>hot</u> or <u>exercising</u> you need to drink <u>more</u> to get enough water into your system.

6) <u>Overhydration</u> can also be very <u>serious</u>. It's caused by drinking <u>huge amounts of water</u> in a <u>short period of time</u>, leading to headaches, nausea and confusion. It also <u>dilutes</u> the concentration of <u>nutrients</u> in our blood — this can affect the function of organs like the <u>kidneys</u>, which in some cases can be fatal.

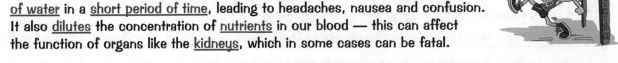

Fibre Optics — a range of light snacks to aid digestion...

Don't get confused — while fibre isn't digested by the body, it plays a very important role in our digestive system.

Q1   State two ways in which water can be lost from the body.   [2 marks]

Healthy Eating Guidelines

The <u>government</u> issues <u>guidelines</u> on healthy eating. Crunch some lettuce while you read all about it.

The Eatwell Guide Gives Recommendations for a Healthy Diet

The <u>Eatwell Guide</u> is an easy way of showing <u>how much</u> or little of each <u>food group</u> is recommended.

Fruit and vegetables:

- About <u>1/3</u> of your daily food intake.
- Aim to eat at least <u>5 portions</u> of <u>fruit and veg</u> every day.

One portion is:

- <u>One piece</u> of <u>medium-sized</u> fruit, e.g. apple, banana or orange.
- <u>One heaped tablespoon</u> of <u>dried fruit</u>, e.g. raisins, sultanas.
- <u>Three heaped tablespoons</u> of <u>cooked vegetables</u>, e.g. carrots, sweetcorn.
- 150 ml of <u>fruit juices</u> or <u>smoothies</u> (only <u>one glass</u> per day).

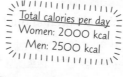

Total calories per day
Women: 2000 kcal
Men: 2500 kcal

Starchy carbohydrates:

- About <u>1/3</u> of your daily food intake*.
- Choose <u>higher fibre</u>, <u>wholegrain</u> options with less <u>fat</u>, <u>sugar</u> and <u>salt</u>.
- Try to include a <u>starchy</u> food in <u>every meal</u>. E.g. <u>potatoes</u>, <u>wholegrain bread</u> and <u>cereals</u> and <u>spaghetti</u>.

*Careful here — we're talking about the <u>amount of carbs</u> you eat, not how much energy you get from them (p.16).

Oils and spreads:

- Use <u>unsaturated oils</u> and <u>spreads</u>, and not very often. E.g. <u>sunflower</u> and <u>olive</u> oil.

Beans, pulses, fish, meat and other protein:

- Aim to eat <u>two portions</u> of <u>fish</u> a week (one <u>oily</u>, e.g. <u>salmon</u>, <u>sardines</u>).
- <u>Pulses</u> are a <u>good alternative</u> to meat.
- Choose <u>lean cuts</u> of meat and eat less <u>processed meat</u> (e.g. <u>bacon</u>, <u>sausages</u>).

Dairy products and alternatives:

- Have <u>some dairy</u> and try <u>lower fat</u> options, e.g. <u>1% fat milk</u>, or <u>reduced-fat cheese</u>.
- You can also try dairy alternatives, such as <u>soya</u> or <u>rice-based milks</u>.

You should also:

 Drink <u>6-8 glasses</u> of <u>fluids</u> a day — hydration is part of a healthy diet.
But no more than one glass of fruit juice a day.

 Eat less <u>sugary</u>, <u>salty</u> and <u>fatty</u> foods, e.g. <u>muffins</u>, <u>cakes</u>, <u>biscuits</u>.
We should aim for no more than 6 g of salt a day.

If only custard creams were 1 of your 5 a day...

This stuff is really important — try covering up the Eatwell Guide and see if you can sketch your own from memory.

Breakfast: Wholemeal toast & jam
Lunch: Egg & cheese sandwich, crisps, chocolate, yoghurt
Dinner: Chicken curry & rice, cream cake.

Q1 Peter has a list of the food that he ate for breakfast, lunch and dinner.

    a) Describe to what extent Peter meets the guidelines set out in the Eatwell Guide. [3 marks]

    b) Suggest an alternative, healthier dessert for Peter's dinner. [1 mark]

Nutritional Needs of Different Age Groups

Everyone should roughly aim to follow the healthy eating guidelines, but our nutritional needs change throughout each stage of our lives. These pages will give you the low-down.

Children Grow Quickly and need Lots of Energy

Young Children (2-5 years old)

1) Between 2 and 5 years old, children should gradually move to a diet based on the Eatwell Guide.

2) Young children do not have large stomachs, so they should have small and frequent meals to get the energy they need.

   ...although it's better to get calcium from a range of foods.

3) Milk is an important source of nutrients — 300 ml each day gives young children the daily calcium they need and it's also a good source of vitamin A.

4) Young children should be frequently encouraged to try a variety of foods. Kids can be dead fussy though, so experiment mixing new foods with things they like and offer them different choices.

Children (5-12 years old)

1) Children grow quickly and are very active, so there is an extra demand for energy and nutrients — they need more than adults (in proportion to their body size).

2) Good amounts of these nutrients are important for children:

Nutrient	Reason	Example Foods
Protein	To help them grow and repair the body.	Fish fingers, boiled eggs
Carbohydrate	Starchy carbohydrates and some fats provide energy for growth and physical activity. Saturated fats should be eaten in moderation.	Mashed potato, pasta
Fat		Peanuts, avocados
Calcium	For healthy teeth and bone development.	Milk, yoghurt tubes, cheese
Vitamin D		Tuna, salmon

3) Foods high in sugar should be eaten infrequently, and only ever at mealtimes. Too many of these foods can cause tooth decay and weight gain.

4) Eating habits of children may be adopted from their parents, so families should eat healthily together.

Teenagers

1) Teenagers should aim for a balanced diet, according to the Eatwell Guide.

2) Rapid growth spurts happen around the early teens — girls usually start these earlier than boys.

3) Good amounts of these nutrients are important for teenagers:

Nutrient	Reason	Example Foods
Protein	To cope with growth spurts. Boys tend to need more protein than girls as muscular tissue develops.	Omelettes, chicken
Iron	Teenage girls lose iron when they have their period so it needs to be replaced or they could become anaemic (p.14). Vitamin C helps the body absorb the iron.	Spinach, beef
Vitamin C		Peppers, strawberries
Calcium	The skeleton grows quickly during this time. These nutrients are necessary as they help the skeleton reach peak size and bone density.	Milk, yoghurt, kale, tofu
Vitamin D		Tuna, salmon, mackerel

4) During the teen years there can be lots of stress (e.g. exams, media pressure) which affect eating habits — stress can lead to conditions like anorexia, but also overeating which can cause obesity.

Nutritional Needs of Different Age Groups

Here are some more life stages that you have to look forward to. You may as well start planning now...

Adults Stop Growing and Nutritional Needs Don't Vary Much

Adults

1) Growth and development stops, so adults should focus on maintaining a healthy lifestyle — they are encouraged to follow the Eatwell Guide to keep the body disease-free.

2) Men usually require more calories than women because they have more lean muscle (muscles require lots of energy to function properly) and are generally taller and larger.

3) Iron is especially important for adult women as they continue to lose it through periods.

4) Calcium and vitamin D are important for all adults to reduce the chance of bone diseases in later life — women can quickly lose bone strength after the menopause in their 40s or 50s too, so these nutrients are needed to keep the skeleton strong.

5) During pregnancy, women should adapt their diet to help the baby. Pregnant women should:

- eat about 200 more calories per day towards the end of the pregnancy to support the baby's growth. They should be careful not to overeat as it can cause excessive weight gain.
- consume more folic acid — it helps to reduce the risk of birth defects such as spina bifida.

Elderly Adults

1) As we age, our muscle turns into fat, and so our body needs less energy for maintenance.

2) Elderly adults need to take great care with their energy intake — cutting down on excess saturated fats will help avoid health risks like coronary heart disease (see next page).

3) The senses of taste and smell change, which can affect the enjoyment of food. Recipes and meals need to be adapted to make them appealing and interesting.

4) Elderly adults have similar nutritional requirements to younger adults, but they must make sure they get enough:

Nutrient	Reason	Example Foods
Calcium	To help stop bones becoming weak and brittle and reduce the risk of developing bone diseases.	Milk, yoghurt, kale, sardines
Vitamin D		Tuna, salmon, mackerel
Vitamin B12	To keep the brain healthy and prevent memory loss.	Milk, fish, beef
Fibre	To help prevent constipation as the digestive system begins to weaken.	Lentils, wholemeal bread
Vitamin A	To help maintain good eyesight.	Liver, scrambled eggs

5) Vitamin supplements are useful if your diet doesn't contain enough, e.g. less active elderly adults may not get enough vitamin D from sunlight, so may benefit from vitamin D tablets.

Oh, I thought supplements helped you be more flexible...

In the exam you might be asked to plan a meal for a certain age group — although nutrients are important throughout our lives, you need to pinpoint why your meal would benefit that age group in particular.

Q1   Explain the importance of each nutrient for the groups listed below:

    a) Calcium for children   [1 mark]

    b) Protein for teenagers   [1 mark]

    c) Folic acid for pregnant women   [1 mark]

    d) Vitamin B12 for elderly adults   [1 mark]

Diet-Related Health Problems

A <u>bad diet</u> will affect your <u>health</u>, and certain <u>diseases</u> affect your <u>nutritional needs</u>.

Obesity is when the Body has Too Much Fat

1) Obesity is <u>very common</u> — it affects roughly <u>one</u> in every <u>four</u> adults in the UK.

2) <u>Body Mass Index</u> (BMI) is often used to check if someone is overweight or obese.

3) For adults, a BMI between <u>18.5</u> and <u>25</u> is classed as a <u>healthy weight</u>, between <u>25</u> and <u>30</u> as <u>overweight</u>, between <u>30</u> and <u>35</u> as <u>obese</u> and above <u>35</u> as <u>extremely obese</u>.

BMI is not always a reliable indicator of someone's body fat — a person could weigh a lot
(and have a high BMI) due to a large amount of muscle mass rather than body fat.

Causes

- An <u>incorrect balance of energy</u> — a person consumes <u>more</u> <u>calories</u> than they can <u>burn off</u>.
- Eating lots of <u>food</u> high in <u>fat</u> and <u>sugar</u>.
- Having a <u>sedentary lifestyle</u>.

A sedentary lifestyle is one with little or no physical activity.

Health Problems

- <u>High blood pressure</u> and <u>high cholesterol</u> increase the chance of <u>coronary heart disease</u> (see below) and <u>strokes</u>.
- There's a <u>greater risk</u> of developing other <u>serious</u> health conditions such as <u>type 2 diabetes</u> and <u>cancer</u>.
- <u>Breathing difficulties</u>, <u>tiredness</u> and <u>low self-esteem</u> are all common.

Coronary Heart Disease is caused by Clogged Arteries

1) Your <u>cardiovascular system</u> consists of your <u>heart</u> and <u>blood vessels</u>.

2) <u>Coronary heart disease (CHD)</u> is when the <u>coronary arteries</u> (which <u>supply</u> the heart with blood full of <u>oxygen</u>) are <u>narrowed</u>, because they are <u>filled</u> with <u>fatty deposits</u>.

Causes

- Eating lots of <u>saturated fats</u>.
- Being <u>physically inactive</u> — because <u>exercise</u> keeps the heart and the <u>cardiovascular system</u> healthy.
- <u>Smoking</u> — damages the lining of <u>arteries</u> and reduces the oxygen in the blood.
- High <u>blood pressure</u>.

Health Problems

- Blood cannot pass through your blood vessels <u>efficiently</u>, which causes a <u>squeezing pain</u> in your chest (<u>angina</u>) and other areas of your body.
- <u>Blood clots</u> can form which suddenly block <u>blood flow</u> to the heart muscle — the heart doesn't get enough <u>oxygen</u>, which can cause a <u>heart attack</u> (which can be <u>fatal</u>).

<u>Blood pressure</u> is how much pressure the blood puts against the walls of your <u>arteries</u>. High blood pressure puts <u>strain</u> on <u>blood vessels</u> and <u>organs</u> and can increase the risk of <u>heart disease</u> and <u>strokes</u>.

Anaemia can be caused by Iron Deficiency

1) <u>Iron</u> is needed to make <u>red blood cells</u> — these cells carry <u>oxygen</u> from the lungs and travel in your blood around the body to where it is needed.

2) People with <u>anaemia</u> have a <u>reduced amount</u> of <u>red blood cells</u>.

Causes

- Not eating enough <u>iron-rich foods</u>, e.g. <u>red meat</u> and <u>dark green leafy vegetables</u>.
- Women lose iron during their <u>periods</u>.
- <u>Pregnant women</u> lose iron to their baby during pregnancy.

Health Problems

- <u>tiredness</u>
- <u>pale complexion</u>
- <u>heart palpitations</u>
- <u>headaches</u>
- abnormal <u>fingernails</u>

Warning: iron deficiency.

Diet-Related Health Problems

Oh, there's another page on this? Sorry, you just can't get away with having a <u>poor diet</u> scot-free.

Diabetes lets your Blood Glucose Levels run Out of Control

1) <u>Insulin</u> is a <u>hormone</u> that allows <u>glucose</u> to be <u>absorbed</u> by cells in the body.

2) Insulin is created in the <u>pancreas</u> — if there is <u>too much glucose</u> in the blood, the pancreas <u>produces</u> insulin to <u>reduce</u> the <u>blood glucose level</u>.

3) <u>Type 2 diabetes</u> is a disorder where blood glucose levels stay too high because the pancreas either can't <u>produce enough insulin</u> or the <u>body resists it</u>.

> There are two types of diabetes — <u>type 1</u> and <u>type 2</u>. You'll only need to learn about type 2.

Causes

- Being <u>overweight</u> or <u>obese</u>.
- <u>Excessive sugar</u> in the diet can lead to obesity (increasing the risk of type 2 diabetes) — this is affecting more <u>young people</u>.

Health Problems

- Diabetes can cause <u>long-term health problems</u> such as <u>poor eyesight</u> (or even <u>blindness</u>), <u>limb numbness</u>, <u>kidney failure</u> and <u>cardiovascular diseases</u> such as CHD.
- People with diabetes can feel <u>tired</u> and <u>thirsty</u>.
- The body <u>flushes</u> out <u>glucose</u> by <u>passing urine</u> more often.

Poor Diet can Affect the Skeleton too

Your <u>bones</u> and <u>teeth</u> can become <u>diseased</u> if you don't get the <u>right amount</u> of nutrients.

Rickets

- <u>Rickets</u> is a condition that means that the <u>bones</u> are <u>soft</u> and <u>weak</u>.
- This occurs in <u>children</u> if they don't have enough <u>vitamin D</u> or <u>calcium</u> — e.g. little exposure to <u>sunlight</u> or not eating enough <u>foods</u> rich in these nutrients.
- Rickets causes <u>pain</u> in the bones, increases the chances of <u>fracturing bones</u> and can cause physical <u>deformities</u>, e.g. <u>bowed legs</u>.

> Both of these are linked to a lack of vitamin D or calcium — think of some example foods for different age groups that would help prevent these conditions.

Osteoporosis

- Osteoporosis is a <u>bone disease</u> which <u>weakens</u> bones and makes them <u>brittle</u>, increasing the chance of breaking bones from <u>simple falls</u> (called fragility fractures).
- It is <u>common</u> in older people because <u>bone density</u> is lost <u>naturally</u> as we age.
- Women tend to lose bone density <u>more rapidly</u> after the <u>menopause</u>.
- Eating foods rich in <u>vitamin D</u> or <u>calcium</u> can help prevent osteoporosis.

Tooth Decay

- <u>Plaque</u> is a <u>sticky substance</u> that contains lots of <u>bacteria</u> — it <u>builds up</u> on your teeth over time from <u>leftover food</u>.
- Bacteria <u>feed</u> on <u>sugars</u> and create <u>acids</u> that can <u>destroy tooth enamel</u> and cause <u>tooth decay</u> (also called <u>dental caries</u> / <u>cavities</u>).
- <u>Brushing</u> your <u>teeth</u> with <u>fluoride toothpaste</u> twice a day and eating <u>fewer</u> foods <u>high in sugar</u> can help <u>prevent</u> tooth decay.

My cardiovascular system never loved me — such heartache...

Make sure you learn how to prevent diabetes and skeletal problems before covering the pages and scribbling down as much information as possible. Rinse and repeat until you're fluent in diet-related diseases.

Q1 Explain two ways that someone could prevent / reduce the risk of developing:

 a) obesity [2 marks] b) cardiovascular diseases [2 marks]

Energy Needs

You know what we need more of? Acronyms, that's right. <u>BMR</u>, <u>PAL</u> and <u>LOL</u> are all <u>key terms</u> to do with <u>energy</u> and the <u>diet</u> that you'll need to know (alright, I lied about one of them).

BMR is the Minimum Energy needed to Function

1) <u>Basal Metabolic Rate</u> (<u>BMR</u>) is the <u>smallest amount of energy</u> needed for you to stay <u>alive</u> — this is stuff you don't think about, like <u>breathing</u> and keeping your <u>heart beating</u>.

2) These basic <u>life processes</u> can use up to about <u>75%</u> of the energy we use each day — other things like <u>digestion</u> and <u>physical activity</u> make up the rest.

3) There are many <u>factors</u> that affect a person's BMR.

> The average BMR for an adult is about 1500 — 2000 calories.

- <u>Age</u> — BMR <u>decreases</u> as we get older due to <u>reduction</u> of <u>muscle mass</u>.
- <u>Gender</u> — <u>Women</u>, in general, have a <u>lower</u> BMR than men as they're generally smaller and tend to have less muscle.
- <u>Weight</u> and <u>height</u> — <u>Heavier</u> or <u>larger</u> bodies need more <u>calories</u>, so have a <u>higher BMR</u>.
- <u>Exercise</u> — Again, it's all about the <u>muscle</u> — <u>regular exercise</u> (especially <u>strength training</u>) increases <u>muscle</u>, which <u>raises</u> your BMR.

PAL is a way to Express your Physical Activity

Competitive gymnast
PAL = about 2.0

1) Your <u>Physical Activity Level</u> (<u>PAL</u>) is a measure of how active you are/how much exercise you get.

2) If you are more <u>active</u>, e.g. a <u>competitive gymnast</u>, you will have a <u>higher PAL</u> than someone with a <u>sedentary</u> lifestyle.

3) BMR and PAL <u>multiplied together</u> give your <u>daily energy requirement</u>:

> Daily energy requirement (kcal) = BMR × PAL

CGP editor
PAL = about 1.6

4) You have to <u>balance</u> your <u>energy intake</u> to maintain a <u>healthy weight</u>.
- If you consume <u>more</u> energy than you use you will <u>gain weight</u>.
- If you consume <u>less</u> energy than you use you will start to <u>lose weight</u>.

Have the Right Balance of Energy Sources

<u>Carbohydrates</u>, <u>fats</u> and <u>proteins</u> are our main <u>sources of energy</u>.

According to government guidelines, they should be consumed in a certain <u>ratio</u>:

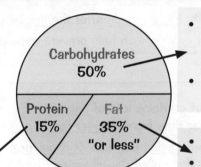

- Try to get a good variety, if eating <u>low biological value proteins</u> (p.1).

- The <u>majority</u> should come as <u>starches</u> and <u>sugars</u> present in milk (<u>lactose</u>) and fruit (<u>fructose</u>).
- No more than <u>5%</u> should come from <u>sugar</u> added to processed foods.

- Getting less than <u>35%</u> is fine.
- Try to <u>limit</u> consumption of <u>saturated fats</u>.

How to increase your PALs — go to lots of parties...

Know your BMR from your PAL and learn how to calculate how much energy we should consume each day.

Q1 Why do men usually have a greater BMR than women? [2 marks]

Q2 How does obesity affect BMR? [2 marks]

Q3 Clive has a BMR of 2000 calories and a PAL of 1.5.
How many calories should he consume per day to maintain his weight? [1 mark]

Nutritional Analysis

Nutritional analysis is about working out the nutritional content of foods... yup, this first bit is a little mathsy.

Macronutrients Have Different Energy Values

1) Energy can be expressed in kilojoules (kJ) or, more commonly, kilocalories (kcal) — when people talk about calories in food, they're usually referring to kilocalories.

2) 1 gram of each major macronutrient (fat, protein and carbohydrate) gives us the approximate energy values shown in the table.

3) If you know how many grams of each macronutrient are in a food, you can calculate its total energy value:

Macronutrient	Energy value (kcal)
Fat (1 g)	9
Protein (1 g)	4
Carbohydrate (1 g)	4

EXAMPLE: A boiled egg contains 7 g fat, 9 g protein and 0.6 g of carbohydrate.

To calculate the total energy value of the egg, look at the table to find the energy value for 1 g and multiply it by how many grams of each macronutrient there are.

Macronutrient content		Energy value	Total energy value
Fat	7 g	7 × 9 = 63 kcal	63 + 36 + 2.4 = 101.4 kcal
Protein	9 g	9 × 4 = 36 kcal	
Carbohydrate	0.6 g	0.6 × 4 = 2.4 kcal	

Use Reference Tables and Software to Find Nutritional Data

Fortunately, you won't have to calculate the energy value of each ingredient — there's loads of nutritional data available out there for both energy and nutritional values, you just need to know where to find it.

1) Packaged foods have to include nutritional labels on their packaging by law (p.46).

2) Reference tables of nutrients for different foods can be found in books or online:

- Foods are listed alphabetically or by food group.

- The nutritional values are usually given per 100 g or per portion of the food...

- ...which means you can't just use these figures as they are. E.g. if you use 10 g of garlic in a recipe, you'll need to divide the values in its row by 10 to give the nutritional value for just 10 g.

Value per 100g	Energy (kcal)	Protein (g)	Carbohydrates (g)	Sugars (g)	Fat (g)	of which saturates	Fibre (g)
Garlic, raw	150	6	30	1	0.5	0.1	2
Gooseberries	45	1	10	8	0.5	0.1	4
Gouda, cheese	350	25	2	2	28	18	0

3) You can also use nutritional analysis software on a computer:

- It lets you input the ingredients of a recipe, and the weight of each.

- It calculates the energy and the amount of nutrients present in the entire meal, and if the recipe serves multiple people, you can find the nutritional content per portion.

- It can have additional features such as comparing nutritional values to the recommended amounts for different ages.

  "Explore food" is a free nutritional analysis tool you can try online — visit http://explorefood.foodafactoflife.org.uk/ for more info.

Mashed potato coats — the latest in food soft-wear.

Nutritional Analysis

Whoopie — you can look up and work out the energy and nutritional information of foods... so what?
Well, armed with this data you can suggest and change ingredients to make meals more healthy and balanced.

Modify Meals to follow Healthy Eating Guidelines

You should refer to the Eatwell Guide (p.11) when creating your recipes — you can change ingredients and
your cooking techniques to follow the guidelines more closely and make meals more nutritionally balanced.

EXAMPLE:

Look at the ingredients in the recipe on the right.
Find the nutritional content of the recipe and modify
the ingredients to meet healthy eating guidelines.

The nutritional values of foods are often given in grams, so
estimate the weight of the lemon juice — 60 ml ≈ 60 g.

Use reference tables or nutritional analysis
software to find the nutritional values for
each ingredient and the whole recipe:

Rhubarb Crumble
(*Serves two*)

Ingredients:
400 g rhubarb
100 g demerara sugar   80 g salted butter
150 g white flour   60 ml lemon juice

Modifying the recipe:

E.g.

Rhubarb Crumble	Energy (kcal)	Protein (g)	Carbohydrates (g)	Sugars (g)	Fat (g)	of which saturates	Fibre (g)
per recipe (~800 g)	1708	16	258	106	68	42	10
per portion (~400 g)	854	8	129	53	34	21	5

The recipe serves two, so you need to
consider the nutrients in each portion.

- Switch to a wholemeal flour to give the
  crumble more fibre and substitute 25 g of
  the flour for oats to give a better texture.

- The sugar content is really high — reduce the
  amount of sugar used to 50 g or use a natural
  alternative sweetener such as stevia or xylitol.

- Add a handful of walnuts to provide extra
  flavour and nutrients (unsaturated fats,
  fibre and vitamins).

- Change the recipe to serve 3 to 4 people instead.

Here are some general suggestions on reducing sugar, salt and saturated fat intake and increasing our fibre:

Reducing Sugar

- Sugar is often 'disguised' as other names
  (e.g. sucrose, corn syrup) on packaging,
  so study nutritional labels carefully.
- Use fewer sugary condiments
  (e.g. ketchup, barbecue sauce).
- Use less sugar when baking.

Reducing Salt

- Use less foods that have salt added to
  preserve or flavour them, e.g. cured meat.
- Create your own sauces and stocks —
  ready-made ones are often very high in salt.
- Use seasonings other than salt to add
  flavour, e.g. ginger or chilli.

Reducing Saturated Fats

- Use low-fat spreads and vegetable oils.
- Eat lean cuts of meat, and grill, bake or
  steam foods instead of frying or roasting.
- Allow fat to drain away when cooking.

Increasing Fibre

- Go for wholemeal bread, flour and pasta.
- Include more beans, lentils (and other
  pulses) and vegetables in meals.
- Keep skins on potatoes.

Want some information on Bacon? Go to an art calorie...

Try experimenting with recipe ideas and use reference tables or software to find how the nutritional value varies.

Q1   Calculate the energy value of a pork pie (30 g fat, 15 g protein and 30 g of carbohydrates).   [2 marks]

Q2   Give three ways you could modify potato chips to make them more nutritionally balanced.   [3 marks]

Planning Meals for Different Groups

There are many <u>factors</u> to consider when planning meals, e.g. <u>costing</u>, <u>portion size</u> and <u>dietary requirements</u>. You need to cater for different <u>ages</u> too — children might not rave about your <u>healthy cabbage soup</u>.

Research the Cost of Ingredients

1) <u>Healthier</u> and more <u>nutritional</u> ingredients are often <u>more expensive</u> — e.g. <u>lean meat</u> (p.57).

2) Buying <u>individual</u> ingredients for a recipe is often <u>cheaper per portion</u> than buying <u>ready-made</u> food, e.g. a <u>pizza</u>. However, you'll usually have to buy <u>more</u> ingredients than you need for the recipe.

3) You can <u>compare</u> the prices of <u>ingredients</u> at <u>different shops</u> (or use <u>comparison websites</u>) and <u>reduce</u> the <u>quantity</u> of <u>expensive ingredients</u> (e.g. <u>cheese</u>, <u>meat</u>) to make your meals <u>cheaper</u>.

4) You can <u>work out</u> the <u>total cost</u> of a meal by working out the cost of each <u>individual ingredient</u> — <u>write down</u> each ingredient and <u>calculate</u> its <u>cost</u> from its <u>weight</u>:

Ingredient	Weight	Cost (per 100 g)	Cost (per ingredient)
Potatoes (500 g)	500 g	£0.10	£0.10 x 5 = £0.50
Butter (20 g)	20 g	£0.40	£0.40 ÷ 5 = £0.08
2 Onions	200 g	£0.06	£0.06 x 2 = £0.12
1 Red Pepper	150 g	£0.50	£0.50 x 1.5 = £0.75
9 Eggs	500 g	£0.30	£0.30 x 5 = £1.50

Spanish omelette (serves 4)

Total cost
£0.50 + £0.08 + £0.12 + £0.75 + £1.50 = £2.95

Cost per portion
£2.95 ÷ 4 = about £0.74

Control your Portion Size

<u>Portion size</u> is <u>important</u> — good portion <u>control</u> means you can avoid <u>overfeeding</u> or <u>underfeeding</u> people. For ingredients and meals you may want to use <u>guidelines</u> and <u>equipment</u> to get the portion size correct:

<u>One portion</u> of <u>meat</u> should be roughly the size of your <u>palm</u>.

<u>One portion</u> of <u>cooked vegetables</u> should be roughly the size of your <u>fist</u>.

Use <u>scoops</u> to measure out the <u>same</u> portion size <u>each time</u>.

Use <u>cutters</u> and <u>dividers</u> to <u>divide</u> pizzas, pies, cakes etc.

Meal Ideas for Different Age Groups

Make sure you plan your meals to be <u>nutritionally balanced</u>, <u>appropriate</u> for the <u>age group</u> (p.12-13) and that any <u>dietary requirements</u> (next page) are catered for. Take a look at these <u>examples</u>:

Children

Ingredients	Nutritional importance
Baked fishcakes	Good source of protein — children need lots of it.
Carrots, peas	Packed with vitamin C (and make up 2 of their 5 a day).
Mashed potato	A starchy carbohydrate that is a healthier alternative to chips. Made with milk so includes calcium needed for healthy teeth and bones.

Make meals for children <u>visually interesting</u> by including different <u>colours</u> and <u>textures</u>.

Teenagers

Ingredients	Nutritional importance
Grilled chicken breast	Protein for rapidly growing bodies.
Wholewheat couscous	Lots of carbohydrate and fibre and low in saturated fat.
Olives, spinach	Both good sources of iron — important for girls so they don't become anaemic.
Red pepper	Adds colour and a good source of vitamin C too.

EXAM TIP:
You might have to modify a recipe to make it more nutritionally balanced — e.g. how could you increase the calcium content here?

Elderly

Ingredients	Nutritional importance
Lentil stew	Pulses are rich in protein and fibre. Fibre helps the weakening digestive system.
Sweet potato	Lots of carotene (vitamin A) — helpful for healthy eyes.
Soft tofu	Is easy to chew and is a good source of calcium to help maintain bone strength.
Wholemeal bread roll	Another good source of fibre — much more than white bread.

Planning Meals for Different Groups

Some people have special dietary requirements — intolerances, allergies and diseases affect what people eat.

Lactose Intolerance

People with lactose intolerance need to avoid food containing a type of sugar called lactose.
Lactose is found in milk, so it's important to check labels for any milk-based ingredients.

- Consider substituting normal milk for a lactose-free milk such as soya or almond milk.
- Dairy products, e.g. cheese and yoghurt, have lactose-free alternatives.

Nut Allergy

People with nut allergies have to avoid nuts and processed foods that may contain traces of them.
Allergic reactions can be fatal, so it's important you check labels very carefully — if you have any
doubts about whether a product contains nuts it's safest not to use it.

- Nuts aren't vital for a balanced diet, so substitutions can be made.
- Some biscuit and cake recipes only use nuts to add flavour, so the nuts can just be removed.

Coeliac Disease

People with coeliac disease cannot eat food containing gluten.
They must avoid wheat, barley and rye and products made with them.

- Many basic foods are fine for a coeliac — meat, vegetables and dairy products are all naturally free of
  gluten and should be included in their normal diet. However, you should check the label just in case.
- Use alternative flours, e.g. coconut, tapioca or rice flours are all gluten-free alternatives to wheat flour.

Vegetarians

A vegetarian is someone who chooses not to eat any meat (and sometimes products derived from animals,
like milk and eggs) due to personal or religious beliefs (p.44). There are different branches of vegetarianism:

- Pescatarians will not eat meat, but will consume fish and animal products, e.g. eggs, cheese and milk.
- Lacto-ovo vegetarians will not eat any meat or fish but will consume milk, eggs and other animal products.
- Lacto vegetarians will not eat any meat, fish or eggs, but will consume milk and other dairy products.
- Vegans will not eat any meat, fish or animal products.

1) Dishes with vegetables are generally healthy and nutritionally balanced, but vegetarians
   will need to get protein from sources other than meat (see p.1).

2) Quorn™ products are popular — they contain mycoprotein which is said to have a texture similar
   to meat. (Most Quorn™ products use egg white, so they are not all suitable for vegans.)

3) Vegetarians should be careful of hidden animal-based ingredients, such as
   gelatine (used in jelly and marshmallows) and rennet (used in cheese).

Snails, snakes, dolphins — all of them lactose...

By now you should be confident in adapting recipes to make them suitable for different groups and know how to
cost things correctly — alternative ingredients (e.g. gluten-free) can often be more expensive than regular foods.

Q1   Adapt these dishes to make them more suitable for each of the following:

   a) Cottage pie for someone with lactose intolerance.   [1 mark]

   b) Chicken and broccoli pasta bake for a vegetarian.   [1 mark]

   c) Apple crumble for someone with coeliac disease.   [1 mark]

Revision Questions for Section One

That's your lot for <u>section 1</u> — make sure you go back to any tricky bits before delving into these questions.
- Try these questions and <u>tick off each one</u> when you <u>get it right</u>.
- When you've done <u>all the questions</u> for a topic and are <u>completely happy</u> with it, tick off the topic.

<u>Protein, Fats and Carbohydrates (p.1-6)</u> ☑

1) Give three reasons our bodies need proteins.
2) Name four 'alternative proteins'.
3) Describe two effects caused by   a) an excess of protein   b) a deficiency of protein
4) Give three reasons our bodies need fats.
5) Explain the difference between saturated and unsaturated fats.
6) Describe four effects caused by   a) an excess of fat   b) a deficiency of fat
7) Describe three effects caused by   a) an excess of carbohydrates   b) a deficiency of carbohydrates

<u>Vitamins, Minerals, Fibre and Water (p.7-10)</u> ☑

8) For each fat-soluble vitamin (A, D, E and K):   a) Give an example of a food it can be found in
    b) Explain why the body needs it   c) Explain a risk of having a deficiency of it
9) List five foods that are rich in B-vitamins.
10) Explain the importance of the following vitamins in our diet:
    a) B1 (thiamin)   b) B2 (riboflavin)   c) B9 (folic acid)   d) B12   e) C (ascorbic acid)
11) Explain the importance of these minerals in our diet:
    a) Calcium   b) Iron   c) Sodium   d) Phosphorous
12) Why is fibre needed for our digestive systems?
13) Explain why it's important to keep the body hydrated.

<u>Healthy Eating Guidelines and Nutritional Needs (p.11-13)</u> ☑

14) Sketch and label each section of the 'Eatwell Guide'.
15) Describe the nutritional needs for a) older children   b) teenagers   c) adults   d) elderly adults

<u>Diet-Related Health Problems (p.14-15)</u> ☑

16) Describe the causes and health problems for the following:
    a) obesity   b) coronary heart disease   c) anaemia   d) type 2 diabetes
17) Explain what the following health problems are and how you could prevent them:
    a) rickets   b) osteoporosis   c) tooth decay

<u>Energy Needs, Nutritional Analysis and Planning Meals (p.16-20)</u> ☑

18) What is: a) basal metabolic rate (BMR)   b) physical activity level (PAL)?
19) According to government guidelines, what percentage of our total energy should come from:
    a) carbohydrates   b) fat   c) proteins?
20) What is nutritional analysis? Where can you find nutritional data?
21) Give one example of how you can modify a recipe to:
    a) reduce sugar   b) reduce salt   c) reduce saturated fat   d) increase fibre
22) Draw a table that could be used to calculate the cost of a recipe.
23) Give two examples of equipment used to control portion size.
24) Plan a meal for each dietary requirement below. Explain why you chose each ingredient.
    a) lactose intolerance   b) nut allergies   c) coeliac disease   d) vegan

Why Food is Cooked

We all love food — heck, we have at least three moments in the day dedicated to it. This section explains <u>why</u> we cook food, the <u>different ways</u> we cook it and the <u>science</u> behind these methods — let's get started...

Food is Cooked for Many Different Reasons

<u>Different cooking methods</u> change our food in <u>different ways</u> — these include changes to <u>appearance</u>, <u>texture</u>, <u>flavour</u>, <u>smell</u> and <u>nutritive value</u>. Below are some of the reasons why we cook — try and keep them in mind as you're reading this section, as lots of the information can be related back to these points:

To make it safe to eat

1) Many food sources (including <u>meat</u>, <u>poultry</u> and <u>eggs</u>) can contain <u>harmful bacteria</u> that can make us ill. Luckily, bacteria can be <u>killed</u> if food is cooked long enough at a <u>high temperature</u> (see p.36).

2) Some foods contain <u>harmful toxins</u> that are <u>destroyed</u> when the food is cooked — e.g. <u>red kidney beans</u> have to be soaked, boiled and simmered before they are safe to eat, crikey!

To improve shelf life

1) When foods are cooked at high temperatures, <u>bacteria</u> and <u>mould</u> are <u>destroyed</u> (see p.36).

2) This is one of the ways that food can be <u>preserved</u> during the manufacturing process.

3) E.g. milk is <u>pasteurised</u> (heated to a high temperature and cooled) — this helps it stay <u>fresh</u> for <u>longer</u>.

To develop flavours

1) <u>Chemical reactions</u> take place during cooking that <u>change</u> the <u>flavour</u> of the food. E.g. <u>caramelisation</u> can occur when onions are cooked, making them taste <u>sweeter</u> (see p.29).

2) <u>Roasting</u> meats and vegetables creates more <u>intense flavours</u>. The food becomes <u>browner</u> and <u>crispier</u> with more <u>fat added</u> to it and as <u>water evaporates</u> from inside the food.

3) Cooking also allows the flavours of <u>different foods</u> to <u>combine</u>, e.g. when braising a meat in a pot of <u>liquid</u> and <u>veg</u> (see p.25).

To improve texture

1) Cooking usually makes it <u>easier</u> for us to <u>chew</u>, <u>swallow</u> and <u>digest</u> our food.

2) Some foods become <u>softer</u> when they're cooked. E.g. vegetables like broccoli and carrots become <u>more flexible</u> and foods like rice and pasta swell as their <u>starch molecules soften</u> (see p.29).

3) Meats become more <u>tender</u> (softer, more succulent and easier to chew) as <u>solid fats</u> in the food <u>melt</u> and <u>proteins soften</u>.

4) Other foods become <u>firm</u> when they're cooked. E.g. the <u>proteins</u> in egg whites <u>coagulate</u> (see p.28) — this turns the food <u>opaque</u> and more <u>solid</u>.

5) However, meats can become <u>tough</u> and egg whites <u>rubbery</u> if they are <u>overcooked</u>.

6) A change in texture can also make food <u>more pleasant</u> to eat — e.g. roast potatoes have a <u>soft centre</u> but a <u>crispy outside</u>, and baked bread has a <u>light-textured</u> inside but a <u>crusty</u> outside.

To give variety in the diet

1) Foods can be cooked in <u>different ways</u> to create <u>variety</u>.

2) For example, if you had a craving for beef you could satisfy it with <u>grilled steak</u>, <u>roast beef</u>, <u>beef stew</u>, <u>pan-fried minced beef</u> for a spaghetti Bolognese or a <u>barbecued burger</u> to name only a few.

My vegetarian friend had this really bad nightmare...

Food Science? I think it's thyme to raise the stakes...

Changing the flavour, texture and smell of our food is all about making it more palatable (appealing) — if I had the choice between a delicious, tender roast chicken or a tasteless, tough one I know which I would choose.

Q1   Explain why chicken must be cooked before it is eaten.   [2 marks]

Heat Transfer

Now it's time for a page of hard-boiled science — it's all about the different ways we use heat when cooking.

Heat can be Transferred in Three Different Ways

Food is cooked using heat energy. Transferring heat energy means moving it from one place to another — this happens in three different ways:

Conduction

1) Conduction is the transfer of heat energy through the vibration of particles.

2) In a solid, the particles are held tightly together. So when one particle vibrates, it bumps into other particles nearby and quickly passes the vibrations on.

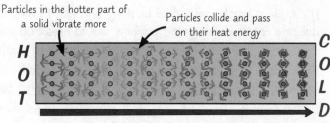

Particles in the hotter part of a solid vibrate more

Particles collide and pass on their heat energy

H O T   **C O L D**

Heat flows in this direction through the solid.

3) When a pan is placed on a hob, heat energy from the hob causes particles in the pan to vibrate more and gain heat energy.

4) When these particles collide with nearby particles, they pass some of their extra heat energy on to them.

5) This process continues throughout the pan until the heat has passed all the way through.

6) When food is placed into the hot pan, heat energy is transferred from the particles in the pan to the particles in the food in a similar way until the food is cooked through.

7) Metals are good conductors of heat. This is why most pans are made out of metal — so energy from the cooker is quickly transferred to the pan and its contents.

Convection

1) Convection is the transfer of heat energy through gases (e.g. air) or liquids.

2) When you heat up a liquid, the liquid near the heat source warms up faster.

3) The warmer liquid rises above its colder surroundings — like a hot air balloon does.

4) As the warm liquid rises, colder liquid takes its place.

5) This colder liquid is heated and when it starts to rise, colder liquid takes its place.

6) As this process continues, you end up with a circulation of fluid (convection currents) — after a while, this circulation of heat results in the whole fluid being heated.

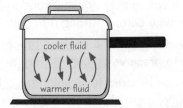

cooler fluid

warmer fluid

7) Convection also occurs in ovens — hot air rises and cooler air falls in the same way.

Radiation

1) Radiation is the transfer of heat energy through waves of radiation — it's like how radiation from the Sun heats up the Earth.

2) Unlike conduction and convection, there is no direct contact between the heat source and the food.

3) Cookers like grills and toasters use radiation to cook food.

4) They emit waves of radiation — when these waves reach the food, they are absorbed and heat the food up.

Bread being toasted. The glowing heating elements emit radiation.

5) Microwaves use radiation to heat up the fat, sugar and water molecules in our food.

Metals are good conductors — but what about Henry Wood?

Rather than using these heat transfer methods separately, we often use a combination of them when we cook.

Q1   Explain the methods of heat transfer used to bring a pan of water to the boil.   [4 marks]

Cooking Methods — Water-Based

I don't know about you, but all this talk of cooking is starting to make me feel just a tiny bit <u>peckish</u>...

Water is used to Cook in Lots of Different Ways

Boiling

- Boiling involves cooking food by heating it in a pan of <u>boiling liquid</u>, usually <u>water</u>.
- The types of food that are boiled include: tougher cuts of <u>meat</u>, <u>potatoes</u>, <u>rice</u>, <u>pasta</u> and <u>veg</u>.

- It's quite a <u>harsh</u> method of cooking and can't be used on delicate foods because the bubbles would break up the food — <u>over-boiling</u> can also make foods like pasta <u>too soft</u>.
- Boiling is a <u>healthy</u> way to cook as <u>no fat</u> is added. However, if veg is boiled for too long, <u>colour</u>, <u>flavour</u> and <u>water-soluble vitamins</u> (see p.8) are <u>lost</u> in the water.
- Boiled food is often not as <u>tasty</u> / <u>attractive</u> as food cooked by methods like roasting.
- However, boiling foods in a small amount of water with a <u>lid</u> covering the pan uses <u>less energy</u> than other methods, e.g. roasting or simmering.

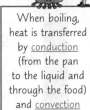

> When boiling, heat is transferred by <u>conduction</u> (from the pan to the liquid and through the food) and <u>convection</u> (through the liquid).

> You can use the water from boiled food to make a tasty and nutritious stock or gravy.

Steaming

- Steaming means cooking food with <u>steam</u> from <u>boiling water</u> or <u>stock</u>.
- Foods you can steam include: <u>fish</u>, <u>rice</u> and <u>vegetables</u>.

- <u>No fat</u> is added and because there is <u>no direct contact</u> with <u>water</u>, the veg keep more of their <u>taste</u>, <u>texture</u>, <u>colour</u> and <u>nutrients</u> than if they'd been boiled — this makes it the <u>healthiest</u> way to cook. However, food may not have as much <u>flavour</u> compared to, say, <u>fried</u> or <u>roasted</u> food.
- Steaming is a <u>gentle</u> way to cook — so it's a good method for <u>delicate</u> foods such as fish, but not for tough meats.

> When steaming, heat is transferred through <u>conduction</u> (from the pan to the water and through the food) and <u>convection</u> (through the steam).

Blanching

- Blanching involves <u>part-cooking</u> food in <u>boiling water</u> for a very short time before putting it in <u>cold</u> (or iced) <u>water</u>.
- The cold water <u>stops</u> the <u>cooking process</u> — this helps to preserve <u>colour</u>, <u>texture</u> and <u>vitamins</u>.
- Blanching can be used to <u>remove harsh flavours</u> in food, e.g. <u>raw onions</u> are blanched to give them a <u>milder taste</u>.
- Blanching foods like <u>tomatoes</u> and <u>almonds</u> makes their skins shrivel up, making the skins much <u>easier to remove</u>.
- It's also used to prepare <u>fruit</u> & <u>veg</u> for <u>freezing</u> (see p.35).

Simmering

- Simmering is like boiling, but more <u>gentle</u> as the <u>temperature</u> is slightly <u>lower</u> than boiling point (but still higher than when poaching).
- It's a very common cooking method for <u>soups</u> and <u>curries</u>.
- Simmering <u>preserves</u> more <u>nutrients</u> than boiling.

Poaching

- Poaching involves cooking food in a pan of liquid <u>below boiling point</u>, usually around <u>80 °C</u>.
- The types of food that are poached include: <u>eggs</u>, <u>fruit</u> and <u>fish</u>.
- Poaching is a <u>gentle</u> way to cook and it helps keep the food <u>tender</u>.
- Like with boiling, <u>nutrients</u> and <u>flavours</u> are transferred to the liquid, lowering the <u>nutritional content</u> and <u>tastiness</u> of the food.
- However, if food is poached in a <u>tasty sauce</u> (e.g. fish poached in a white sauce), the food can absorb <u>flavours</u> and give <u>variety</u>.

> When poaching, heat is transferred through <u>conduction</u> (from the pan to the liquid and through the food) and <u>convection</u> (through the liquid).

Cooking Methods — Water-Based and Fat-Based

Braising

- Braising involves <u>slowly</u> cooking food in an ovenproof pot that has the lid on and contains <u>liquid</u> (usually water, stock or wine) and often <u>herbs</u> and <u>vegetables</u>.
- Food is cooked in the covered pot by a mixture of <u>simmering</u> and <u>steaming</u>.
- It's a great method for <u>big</u> or <u>tough</u> joints of <u>meat</u> because the gentle cooking of the meat helps to <u>tenderise</u> it.
- Before meat is braised, it's usually lightly fried to <u>brown</u> and <u>seal</u> it — this helps to keep <u>juices</u> inside the meat and gives it a <u>caramelised</u> flavour (see p.29).
- The <u>flavours</u> from the <u>liquid</u> and any <u>vegetables</u> and herbs in the pot are also <u>absorbed</u> by the joint — tasty.

When braising, heat is transferred through <u>conduction</u> (from the dish to the liquid and through the food) and <u>convection</u> (through the liquid and steam).

Frying uses Hot Fat or Oil to Cook Food

When frying, <u>fat</u> or <u>oil</u> is heated to a <u>very high temperature</u>. Different types of frying use <u>different amounts</u> of <u>fat</u>:

Hot oil or fat can cause <u>serious burns</u>, and it's <u>highly flammable</u> — so using a large amount can be dangerous.

When frying, heat is transferred to the food by <u>conduction</u> (from the pan to the fat and through the food).

Stir-Frying

- Stir-frying tends to be done in a <u>wok</u> (a large round-based frying pan) coated in a <u>small amount</u> of oil, making it pretty healthy.
- Stir-fried foods include <u>noodles</u>, <u>vegetables</u>, <u>tofu</u> and small pieces of <u>meat</u> and <u>fish</u>.
- Food cooks <u>very quickly</u> and needs to be <u>moved</u> around the wok all the time so it doesn't burn — because they're cooked quickly, <u>vegetables</u> keep <u>more</u> of their <u>nutrients</u>.
- Stir-fried meals tend to have <u>more vegetables</u> than meat (some use no meat at all), making them a <u>healthy option</u>.

Stir-frying and shallow frying both increase the <u>flavour</u> of food because some of the fat is <u>absorbed</u> by the food as it cooks. Foods like onions also <u>caramelise</u> when they're fried, making them taste <u>sweeter</u> (see page 29).

Shallow Frying

- Shallow frying uses a frying pan coated in a <u>medium amount</u> of fat or oil.
- Shallow-fried foods include: <u>meat</u> (like chops, bacon and sausages), <u>fish</u>, <u>eggs</u> and <u>pancakes</u>.
- <u>More fat</u> is used when shallow frying than stir frying, so it's a <u>less healthy</u> method of cooking. Solid fats in the food also <u>melt</u> into the pan as the food cooks, increasing the amount of fat in the pan even more.
- Shallow frying gives foods a <u>crispier texture</u> than stir-frying.

Another fat-based method of cooking is <u>sweating</u>. This method <u>releases moisture</u> from food, making it more <u>tender</u> and <u>sweet-tasting</u>. Sweating is most often used for <u>vegetables</u> such as onions, and uses a <u>small amount of oil</u> over a <u>low heat</u> — it's this low heat that allows the food to release moisture <u>without browning</u>. While the food is sweating, it's usually <u>covered with a lid</u> to help the moisture (in the form of steam) <u>circulate</u> around the food.

Hey — you're really steaming through this...

One of the key things to remember is that the longer you cook using a water-based method, the more water-soluble vitamins (B & C) are transferred from the food to the water. This lowers the nutritional value of the food — not good.

Q1   Describe one method you could use to cook a tough piece of meat. Explain your choice.   [3 marks]

Q2   Explain the benefits of steaming over other water-based methods of cooking.   [3 marks]

Cooking Methods — Dry Methods

Here are two more pages of <u>cooking methods</u> for you to sink your teeth into. These pages focus on the <u>dry methods</u> of cooking: <u>baking</u>, <u>roasting</u>, <u>grilling</u> and <u>dry frying</u> — is anyone else's stomach grumbling right now?

Baking uses Dry Heat to Cook Food

1) Baking cooks food using <u>dry heat</u>, usually in an <u>oven</u>.

2) Lots of different types of food can be baked, including:

- <u>bread</u>, <u>pastries</u>, <u>cakes</u>, <u>pies</u> and <u>tarts</u>
- <u>potatoes</u>
- whole <u>fishes</u>, like sea bass or salmon

3) <u>Meat</u> is also baked, e.g. in meatloaf or casseroles, although <u>large pieces</u> of meat are usually <u>roasted</u> (see next page).

4) Because <u>hot air rises</u>, the <u>top</u> of an oven is often <u>hotter</u> than the bottom — that's why food cooks <u>quicker</u> on the top shelf than on the bottom shelf.

> Heat is transferred around an oven by <u>radiation</u> and <u>convection</u>, and through the food by <u>conduction</u>.

Baking food like fish or potatoes inside foil helps to keep the moisture in, making them nice and tasty.

5) Modern <u>electric ovens</u> are usually <u>fan-assisted</u> (or "<u>convection ovens</u>") — they have a fan inside that helps to <u>circulate</u> the hot air around the oven. They're much more useful because...

- food bakes more <u>evenly</u> because all parts of the oven are at a <u>similar temperature</u>.
- the oven <u>heats up quicker</u> and your food <u>cooks quicker</u> — so they use <u>less energy</u>.

Advantages	**Disadvantages**
• A <u>wide variety</u> of food can be baked. • The outside of the food <u>browns</u> and <u>crisps</u> up, which <u>looks</u> and <u>tastes nice</u>. • It's <u>quite healthy</u> because <u>no extra fat</u> is added, and solid fats in the food often leave as the food is baked.	• Baking food can take a <u>long</u> time. • Food can become <u>dried out</u>. • It uses a lot of <u>energy</u> as it requires the oven to be kept at a <u>high temperature</u> for a <u>long time</u>.

Fat can Drip Off Food as It's Grilled

1) Grilling uses a <u>dry heat</u> at a <u>higher temperature</u> than baking or roasting to cook food.

2) As food is grilled, fats <u>drip out</u> of the food and the outside of the food becomes <u>golden</u> and <u>crisp</u>.

3) <u>Barbecuing</u> is similar to grilling, but heat radiates from <u>hot coals</u> and food is cooked at <u>lower temperatures</u> for <u>longer</u>.

4) You can grill many foods, such as: <u>smaller bits of meat</u> (like steaks and sausages), <u>vegetables</u> (like courgettes and aubergines) and <u>cheeses</u> (like halloumi or goats' cheese).

> When grilling, heat is transferred to food through <u>radiation</u> (heat radiation from a grill, or hot coals when barbecuing) or <u>conduction</u> (if using a griddle pan).

In summer, we often grill food on a barbecue instead of "barbecuing" food in this slow way.

Advantages	**Disadvantages**
• Food cooks <u>quickly</u> at a high temperature. • It's fairly <u>healthy</u> as <u>no fat</u> is <u>added</u> and fat from the food <u>drips off</u> when cooked. • Just like roasting and baking, the golden outside of the food <u>looks</u> and <u>tastes</u> nice, and can have a lovely <u>crispy texture</u>. • Grilling on a <u>barbecue</u> gives food a <u>smoky flavour</u> which is very <u>popular</u>.	• The <u>high heat</u> used when grilling can make it hard to cook the food <u>evenly</u>. • It's easy to <u>burn</u> the food, or to end up with the outside cooked but the inside still <u>raw</u> — this could lead to food poisoning (see p.39). • Handling both raw and cooked meat on a barbecue might lead to <u>cross-contamination</u> (see p.38).

Cooking Methods — Dry Methods

Fat is Added to Food When it's Roasted

1) Like baking, <u>roasting</u> uses dry heat from an <u>oven</u>.

2) Roasting is usually done at a <u>higher temperature</u> than baking, so foods cook and brown more quickly.

3) <u>Fat</u> is often added to the outside of the food, e.g. potatoes or veg, to help it <u>brown</u> and stay <u>moist</u>. Fat can be added or the fat that has melted from the food (e.g. chicken) can be put back on top — this is called <u>basting</u>.

4) Common types of food that are roasted include: <u>large cuts of meat</u> (such as a leg of lamb, a cut of beef or a whole chicken), <u>potatoes</u>, <u>vegetables</u> (e.g. root vegetables, peppers and onions) and <u>chestnuts</u> (on an open fire...)

> Heat is transferred around an oven by <u>radiation</u> and <u>convection</u>, and through the food by <u>conduction</u>.

Advantages
- Extra fat and a high temperature helps to <u>brown</u> and <u>crisp</u> the outside of food, which <u>looks</u> and <u>tastes delicious</u>.
- The fat from roasted meat can be used to <u>cook other food</u>, e.g. potatoes or fried bread.
- Roasted food can be tasty and <u>moist</u>.
- Roasting can produce meat with a <u>rare</u> (undercooked) centre, which a lot of people like.

Disadvantages
- Roasted food isn't always that <u>healthy</u>, as extra <u>fat</u> is often added.
- Just like baking, it takes a <u>long time</u> to roast food and uses a lot of <u>energy</u>.

> Only certain types of meat (e.g. beef steak) can be served rare because of the dangers of food poisoning and parasites (see page 38).

Dry Frying Does Not Use Added Fat

1) Dry frying means cooking food in a pan <u>without fat</u> or <u>oil</u>.

2) You can dry fry foods that contain <u>natural fat</u>, e.g. <u>minced meats</u>, and <u>bacon</u>. As the food heats up, the fats inside the food <u>melt</u> into the pan and begin to cook the food.

3) <u>Nuts</u>, <u>seeds</u> and <u>spices</u> can also be cooked in this way, although this method is usually called "<u>dry roasting</u>". This helps to release oils and bring out more flavour in the food.

4) Using a <u>medium heat</u> is important at the start of cooking to allow the fats to melt <u>without burning</u> the food — when the fat melts, the temperature can be increased as the fat starts to fry the food.

> When dry frying, heat is transferred by <u>conduction</u> (from the cooker to the pan and also through the food).

Advantages
- <u>No extra fats</u> or oils are added, making this method <u>healthier</u> than other frying methods.
- Dry roasting can be used to give a more <u>distinct aroma</u> to <u>nuts</u>, <u>seeds</u> and <u>spices</u>.

Disadvantages
- It takes <u>longer</u> than other frying methods to cook meat thoroughly, because <u>lower temperatures</u> are needed at the start.
- It can only be used for a <u>small range</u> of food types compared to other cooking methods.

Time for a break — my brain is fried after all these methods...

Ahhh, there's nothing quite like the smell of baking wafting through the house... Apparently, a good way to remember something is to associate it with a smell. So get cooking and revising — perfect.

Q1 Give one similarity and one difference between roasting and baking. [2 marks]

Q2 Why is grilling vegetables considered healthier than roasting them? [1 mark]

Changing Properties — Proteins

I hope you like eggs, because they're a great way to look at the functional and chemical properties of proteins. Functional = how they change food, chemical = the science behind these changes. Let's get cracking...

Proteins Denature during Preparation and Cooking

1) Proteins (p.1) have a complex structure. When food is cooked, proteins denature — this means the chemical bonds holding their structure together break down.

2) The proteins unravel and their shape changes — in most cases this is irreversible.

3) Proteins can be denatured in different ways, including:

- Physical agitation (e.g. whisking, beating and kneading)
- Changes in temperature (e.g. heat)
- Acids (e.g. lemon juice and marinades)

— Acidic marinades denature the protein in meat before cooking — this makes the meat more tender before you start cooking it.

protein

Denaturation

Coagulation

Denatured Protein Molecules Coagulate

1) Once they have been denatured, protein molecules collide with other protein molecules and coagulate (join together).

2) During this process, water becomes trapped between the protein molecules.

3) Coagulation also changes the appearance and texture of the food. E.g. egg white turns from a see-through liquid into a white solid, while steak becomes brown, firmer and easier to eat as you cook it.

4) However, if food is overcooked and coagulation happens too much, the protein tightens. This forces water out of the molecules, making it dry and chewy.

When eggs are added to breadcrumb coatings and quiche mixtures, the process of protein coagulation helps hold everything together.

Foams are Formed when Air is Trapped

1) Foams, e.g. chocolate mousse, whipped cream or cappuccino foam, form when gas becomes trapped (aeration) inside liquid.

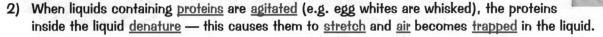

2) When liquids containing proteins are agitated (e.g. egg whites are whisked), the proteins inside the liquid denature — this causes them to stretch and air becomes trapped in the liquid.

3) When the proteins coagulate, this air becomes trapped, creating a foam.

4) However, over-whisking causes these new protein bonds to break — air escapes and the foam collapses.

5) Some foams form a solid structure when they are cooked, e.g. egg white foams become meringues.

Gluten allows Doughs to Stretch and Rise

1) Gluten is a protein found in wheat flours (e.g. those made from wheat, barley and rye).

2) It's formed when water is mixed with the flour to make dough and can be found in foods like bread, pasta, cakes and pastries.

To get a well-risen loaf of bread, it's best to use strong flour because it forms more gluten than other types (e.g. soft flour, which is used more often in cake making).

3) Molecules of gluten are coiled — this means they are able to stretch and bend — this gives all doughs elasticity (stretchiness).

4) Doughs need to be kneaded to 'work' the gluten — this causes gluten strands to get longer, stronger and stretchier.

5) When it reaches a high temperature, gluten coagulates (see above) and the dough stays stretched. This gives foods like well-risen bread a light, airy texture.

Indiana Foams and the Temple of the Whipped Egg White...

It might be ~~fun~~ helpful to draw a mind map of the ways proteins change during cooking — include changes to their chemical properties (e.g. molecules coagulate) and how this affects their functional ones (e.g. food becomes firmer).

Q1   Explain what happens to the protein in egg white when you fry an egg.   [4 marks]

Changing Properties — Carbohydrates

For the exam you'll need to know about <u>three ways</u> in which <u>carbohydrates</u> change in food during cooking. If you need a <u>quick refresher</u> on carbohydrates before we get going, have a quick flick back to <u>pages 5-6</u>.

Starch Gelatinisation Thickens Liquids

1) <u>Gelatinisation</u> helps to <u>thicken</u> foods that contain starch, e.g. <u>sauces</u>, <u>custards</u> and <u>gravies</u>.

2) When <u>starch granules</u> are first mixed with liquid, they become <u>suspended</u> in it — if you don't stir the liquid these granules will sink to the bottom.

3) When the <u>granules</u> are heated with water, the bonds between starch <u>molecules</u> start to break, allowing <u>water molecules</u> to enter. As water is absorbed, the starch granules <u>swell</u> in size and <u>soften</u>.

4) Between <u>62 °C</u> and <u>80 °C</u>, the starch granules <u>burst open</u> and <u>release</u> their <u>starch</u> into the liquid.

5) This release of starch causes the liquid to <u>thicken</u>. How thick the liquid becomes depends on the ratio of starch to liquid in the mixture — the <u>higher</u> the <u>concentration of starch</u>, the <u>thicker</u> the <u>liquid</u>.

6) When it cools, the liquid <u>solidifies</u> and a <u>solid gel</u> is formed — this is useful for making 'set' desserts like <u>custards</u> and <u>lemon pie filling</u>.

Custards can also be set using gelatine or by the process of protein coagulation (see previous page).

7) Gelatinisation also happens when you cook starchy foods like <u>pasta</u> and <u>rice</u> — they swell, soften and release starch into the water as they cook.

Dextrinisation occurs when Starch is Exposed to Dry Heat

1) When starchy foods such as <u>bread</u> or <u>biscuits</u> are cooked with <u>dry heat</u>, e.g. toasting or baking, the <u>starch molecules</u> in the food <u>break down</u> into smaller molecules called <u>dextrins</u>.

2) This breakdown is called <u>dextrinisation</u> and it gives food a <u>browner colour</u> and <u>crispier texture</u> as well as a <u>different taste</u> (imagine the difference in taste between bread and toast).

Random fact: The psychological phenomenon of seeing things in everyday objects (toast, for example) is called pareidolia.

3) The <u>longer</u> the food is cooked, the <u>more starch</u> is converted into <u>dextrin</u> and the darker and crispier the food becomes.

Sugar Caramelises When it's Heated

1) Sugar molecules <u>break down</u> when they reach a <u>high temperature</u> — this causes sugar to turn <u>brown</u> and change <u>flavour</u>. This process is called <u>caramelisation</u>.

2) The sugar goes through various stages:
   - At first the liquid is runny and has a <u>very sweet</u> taste.
   - As time passes, it becomes more like a smooth <u>caramel</u>.
   - Eventually, it turns harder and as it cools it becomes more like a <u>candy</u>.

3) Caramelised sugar can <u>burn</u> very quickly, turning <u>black</u>, <u>brittle</u> and <u>bitter to taste</u>.

4) To avoid this, <u>water</u> is often added during the early stages of heating.

5) Caramelisation gives <u>desserts</u> such as a <u>crème brûlée</u> and <u>apple pie</u> extra sweetness.

6) Even <u>savoury foods</u> that contain <u>sugars</u> (e.g. onions) can <u>caramelise</u>. The sugars in the food are broken down and released, turning the food brown and adding sweetness.

The sugar doesn't actually caramelise until the water has evaporated, but the water helps to increase the temperature of the sugar without it burning.

Tony Starch — saving the world one sauce at a time...

Blimey, there are some long words on this page! While it might be tempting to read over them quickly, it's important you can spell them correctly — especially <u>gelatinisation</u>, <u>dextrinisation</u> and <u>caramelisation</u> — lovely...

Q1 Explain why onions can develop a sweet taste when they are fried in oil or fat. [2 marks]

Q2 Describe what happens to starch granules when they are heated with water. [3 marks]

Changing Properties — Fats and Oils

Fats and oils get a bad rap, but they're actually really useful for a variety of cooking situations...

Fats and Oils Have Lots of Different Uses

Aeration Means Incorporating Air

1) When fats such as butter are beaten with sugar (this process is called creaming) air becomes trapped in the mixture. This air makes the mixture fluffier and lighter in colour.

2) This aeration gives cakes a spongy and light texture when they're cooked.

3) Foods can be aerated in many different ways, e.g. whisking egg whites with a whisk or quickly beating ingredients with a spoon — there's more about this on p.32.

Oils don't trap air as easily as fats — oil-based doughs need something else to add air, e.g. baking powder (see page 32).

Shortening Gives Foods a Crumbly Texture

1) When you rub fat into flour, you cover the flour particles with fat — this gives the flour particles a waterproof coating.

2) This coating prevents long gluten molecules forming when water is added to the flour.

3) This means the dough cannot become stretchy and baked goods like shortbread keep a 'short' (firm and crumbly) texture — hence the name shortening.

4) Shortening is also used when making filled pies and tarts — it's helpful because the base doesn't rise and forms a solid case.

5) Some fats are called 'shortening' — they have 100% fat content (contain no water) which helps stop gluten formation and prevents steam from raising the food.

Lucy was thrilled that her shortening had been successful.

Plasticity Means Ability to be Spread and Shaped

1) Fats have 'plasticity' — we're able to spread and manipulate them.

2) This is possible because fats contain a mixture of different triglycerides (see p.3). These different triglycerides all melt at different temperatures — so fats gradually soften over a range of temperatures rather than melting at just one.

3) The more plasticity a fat has, the easier it is to spread.

Butter can be hard in the fridge, soft at room temperature and melty when it's heated.

4) You'll remember from p.3 that unsaturated fats tend to be soft or liquid at room temperature, while saturated fats tend to be solid — this means that the more unsaturated fatty acids a fat or oil contains, the more plasticity the fat or oil will have (e.g. it will be easier to spread).

5) Plasticity is useful for a range of different reasons, including:

- Decorating cakes with buttercream
- Rubbing fat into flour to make shortened dough (see above)
- Spreading butter on sandwiches and toast
- Putting cream cheese on crackers

An example of taking vegetable fat spread literally...

6) Some vegetable fat spreads are marketed as being 'easy to spread'. This is because they contain a mixture of triglycerides with low melting points, meaning you can spread it as soon as you take it out of the fridge.

Changing Properties — Fats and Oils

We're not quite done with fats and oils yet. Time for the grand finale — emulsions...

Emulsification Keeps Oil and Water in a Stable Emulsion

1) <u>Emulsions</u> are formed when <u>oily</u> and <u>watery liquids</u> are shaken together (the droplets of one spread out through the other).

2) <u>Milk</u>, <u>margarine</u> and <u>mayonnaise</u> are all examples of <u>emulsions</u>.

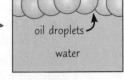

oil droplets

water

3) Usually, oil and water <u>don't mix</u> together and so emulsions <u>separate</u> out again unless you keep shaking or stirring them — or use an <u>emulsifier</u>.

4) The molecules in an <u>emulsifier</u> have <u>two different ends</u>: one is <u>hydrophilic</u> (attracted to water) and the other is <u>hydrophobic</u> (repulsed by water).

hydrophilic head

hydrophobic tail

5) When you add an emulsifier, the <u>water molecules</u> bond to the <u>hydrophilic side</u> and the <u>oil molecules</u> bond to the <u>hydrophobic side</u>. This holds the oil and water together in a <u>stable emulsion</u>, preventing them from separating.

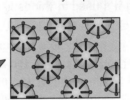

6) Emulsions can either be <u>oil-in-water</u> (e.g. milk, mayonnaise, salad dressings) or <u>water-in-oil</u> (e.g. margarine, butter).

7) <u>Egg yolks</u> contain a natural emulsifier called <u>lecithin</u> (also found in soya) — this is used as the emulsifier in <u>margarine</u> and <u>mayonnaise</u>.

> <u>Mayonnaise</u> is a <u>stable emulsion</u> of <u>egg yolk</u>, oil and vinegar. When making stable emulsions, you need to ensure you add the oil or water <u>gradually</u> and that you <u>mix</u> the ingredients for <u>long enough</u>.

He started it

You Can Use Emulsions for Sauces and Salad Dressings

1) Emulsions are often used as <u>sauces</u> (e.g. mayonnaise) and <u>salad dressings</u> (e.g. vinaigrette).

2) <u>Hollandaise sauce</u> is another example of an emulsion sauce — it's made from butter, water, egg yolks (the <u>lecithin</u> in it acts as an <u>emulsifier</u>) and lemon juice (for flavour).

3) Follow these steps to make a hollandaise sauce:

- <u>Melt</u> the <u>butter</u> in a pan.
- Mix the egg yolks and lemon juice in a bowl.
- <u>Gently warm</u> this mixture by placing the bowl over a pan of simmering water.
- <u>Slowly</u> add the melted butter to the mixture, constantly <u>whisking</u> as you do.
- Keep whisking the sauce until it's all <u>mixed together</u> smoothly.

Note to self: Hollandaise sauce does not go well with apple crumble...

> When making any oil-in-water emulsion, e.g. a sauce or dressing, it's important to <u>add the liquid and emulsifier first</u>, before <u>very slowly</u> adding the oil/fat while mixing vigorously.

My milk carton started leaking — I was overcome with emulsion...

That's it for the functional properties of macronutrients — phew. It's tricky stuff, but make sure you understand it.

Q1   Explain why shortcrust pastry doesn't rise when it's baked.   [5 marks]

Raising Agents

Unless you're craving pancakes, a flat, dense cake is not a good thing — this is why we use <u>raising agents</u>. Raising agents add gas (to doughs and mixtures) which <u>expands when heated</u> to create the rise.

Some Raising Agents Produce Carbon Dioxide...

Don't be fooled — this is no cereal...

Chemical

- When it's heated, <u>bicarbonate of soda</u> breaks down to produce <u>carbon dioxide</u> bubbles that expand to make the mixture <u>rise</u>.
- It has an unpleasant <u>alkaline</u> (soapy) taste, so it needs to be used with a <u>strong flavour</u> to mask it. This is why it's used in things like <u>gingerbread</u> and <u>chocolate cake</u>.
- <u>Baking powder</u> is a mixture of <u>bicarbonate of soda</u> (an alkali) and <u>cream of tartar</u> (an acid). A <u>neutralisation reaction</u> takes place when baking powder is heated which gets rid of the horrid soapy taste.
- <u>Self-raising flours</u> contain a mixture of <u>plain flour</u> and <u>baking powder</u>.

Biological

- <u>Yeast</u> is a <u>biological</u> raising agent used in bread dough.
- It's a <u>microorganism</u> (see p.35) that causes <u>fermentation</u> — a process that releases <u>alcohol</u> and <u>carbon dioxide</u>.
- Doughs containing yeast are often <u>proved</u> (left in a warm place to allow fermentation to take place).
- This stage is important because it's when the carbon dioxide is released and trapped in the dough, causing it to rise — <u>fermentation stops</u> during <u>baking</u> as the yeast is killed by the heat.
- When the dough is baked, the <u>carbon dioxide expands</u>, causing the bread to <u>rise</u> even more — any <u>alcohol</u> produced by the yeast <u>evaporates</u> at this stage.

...Others Add Steam or Air to the Mixture

Steam

- When you use a very hot oven to cook a mixture that deliberately contains a lot of <u>liquid</u> (e.g. <u>batters</u>, <u>puff pastry</u> and <u>choux pastry</u>), water leaves the mixture as <u>steam</u>. As the <u>steam rises</u> it <u>raises</u> the mixture up.
- As the water leaves, the food bakes and becomes more <u>solid</u>. However, it's important to keep the oven door <u>closed</u> or the <u>cold air</u> from outside will cause the mixture to <u>sink</u>.

Mechanical

- We can <u>add air</u> into mixtures with just a little bit of good old-fashioned <u>elbow grease</u>:
- Air can be <u>folded</u> into mixtures and doughs in two different ways:

  1) To "fold" a <u>cake mixture</u>, you <u>carefully</u> use a spoon or spatula to repeatedly <u>pour</u> the liquid mixture over itself — <u>trapping air</u> each time.
  2) <u>Pastry doughs</u> can actually be folded into layers, trapping air <u>in between the layers</u> each time you fold.

- <u>Beating</u> is a more vigorous method where you use a spoon or fork to <u>mix ingredients</u> and <u>quickly</u> drive air into the mixture — e.g. beating eggs and sugar in a mixing bowl.
- <u>Whisking</u> is the same as beating, but you use a <u>whisk</u> instead.
- When you <u>sieve</u> flour, air becomes trapped between the individual <u>flour particles</u>.
- Air is also added when <u>creaming</u>, e.g. creaming butter and sugar, and between flour particles when you <u>rub fat</u> into flour (see p.30).

Learn this stuff — it's the yeast you can do...

Unlike chemical agents which add gas during baking, yeast adds gas to dough before baking. Yeast isn't used in cakes very often because cake mixtures struggle to hold air for the time it takes for fermentation to occur.

Q1   Give two examples of mechanical raising agents.   [2 marks]

Q2   Explain why you would not use bicarbonate of soda to raise a plain sponge cake.   [2 marks]

Revision Questions for Section Two

Congratulations — you've reached the end of <u>section 2</u>. There was a lot of science in there, so well done.
* Try these questions and <u>tick off each one</u> when you <u>get it right</u>.
* When you've done <u>all the questions</u> for a topic and are <u>completely happy</u> with it, tick off the topic.

<u>Why Food is Cooked and Heat Transfer (p.22-23)</u> ☑

1) Give five reasons why food is cooked.
2) Explain in terms of particles how heat is transferred by conduction.
3) Which would be the most suitable material for a frying pan: metal or wood?
4) Explain how convection helps a liquid or gas to be heated.
5) Which method of heat transfer is used when toasting a slice of bread?

<u>Cooking Methods (p.24-27)</u> ☑

6) Boiling and steaming are two water-based methods of cooking.
   a) Which of these methods involves direct contact with food?
   b) Which of these methods produces the more nutritious food?
7) Give one similarity and one difference between simmering and boiling.
8) Give one similarity and one difference between braising and poaching.
9) Explain why food is plunged into cold water during blanching.
10) Give a benefit of poaching over boiling.
11) Which fat-based method of cooking is most suitable for cooking pancakes?
12) Give two advantages of using an oven that's fan-assisted over one that isn't.
13) Explain the difference between grilling and roasting.
14) List the advantages and disadvantages of these cooking methods:
   a) frying   b) baking   c) grilling   d) roasting   e) dry frying

<u>Changing Properties (p.28-31)</u> ☑

15) Give three ways proteins can be denatured.
16) Describe the process of protein coagulation and explain how it affects the texture of food.
17) Explain how foam formation happens in whisked egg whites.
18) What is the name of the protein that gives bread dough its elasticity?
19) Explain how starch can be used to thicken cheese sauce.
20) Name the process that makes biscuits browner and crispier when they're baked.
21) Name and describe the process that takes place when sugar is cooked at a high temperature.
22) What does the term 'aeration' mean?
23) Explain how you can prevent gluten molecules from forming long strands.
24) What is the name given to a fat's ability to be shaped?
25) Explain how emulsifiers can be used to keep oil and water in a stable emulsion.

<u>Raising Agents (p.32)</u> ☑

26) What are the differences between bicarbonate of soda, baking powder and self-raising flour?
27) Name one biological raising agent and explain how it can be used to raise bread dough.
28) Explain how choux pastry profiteroles are risen by steam.
29) Describe six ways you could mechanically incorporate air into a cake mixture.

Food Spoilage

Microorganisms are <u>tiny living things</u> found in <u>air</u>, <u>water</u>, <u>soil</u>, on <u>people</u>... basically <u>everywhere</u>.

Microorganisms Grow in the Right Conditions

<u>Microorganisms</u> include <u>bacteria</u>, <u>moulds</u> and <u>yeasts</u>.
Most are <u>harmless</u>, but <u>pathogenic</u> ones can <u>spoil</u>
food (make it <u>go off</u>) and cause <u>food poisoning</u>.

Pathogenic means something that can produce disease.

Microorganisms need <u>five conditions</u> to grow and <u>multiply</u>:

1)   A <u>warm temperature</u>
2)   Plenty of <u>moisture</u> (water)
3)   Plenty of <u>food</u>
4)   The right <u>pH</u> (not too <u>acidic</u> or <u>alkaline</u>)
5)   Enough <u>time</u> (bacteria split every <u>10-20 minutes</u>)

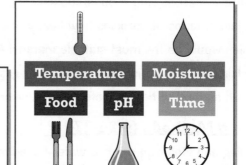

Temperature	Moisture
Food	pH	Time

Changing any <u>one</u> of these <u>conditions</u> will <u>slow</u> or <u>stop</u> the growth of microorganisms altogether.
For example, you could:

• Use a <u>fridge</u> to change the <u>temperature</u> (see p.36).
• <u>Pickle</u> the food in <u>vinegar</u> to change the <u>pH</u>.
• Add <u>salt</u> — salt <u>absorbs water</u> (removes moisture) from the food, <u>drying</u> it out.

High Risk Foods have Ideal Conditions for Bacteria

1)   <u>High risk foods</u> are <u>ready-to-eat</u> foods that, if not <u>stored correctly</u>, could grow <u>harmful bacteria</u>.
2)   They satisfy points <u>2 and 3</u> above — they're <u>moist</u> and <u>high in protein</u> (protein = <u>food</u> for bacteria).

High Risk Foods

1)   <u>cooked meat</u>, <u>fish</u> and <u>poultry</u>
2)   <u>dairy products</u> (<u>eggs</u>, <u>cheese</u>, etc.)
3)   <u>gravies</u>, <u>stocks</u> and <u>sauces</u>
4)   <u>shellfish</u>
5)   <u>cooked</u> rice

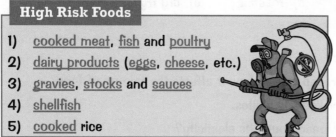

3)   High risk foods have a <u>short shelf life</u>
— you can't keep them for long, or the
bacteria might multiply to <u>dangerous levels</u>.

*The shelf life of a food is the length
of time it can safely be kept for.*

4)   A <u>raw food</u>, e.g. <u>chicken</u>, might have lots of bacteria but it's <u>not</u> classed as a high risk food because you
don't eat it <u>raw</u>. Once it's <u>cooked</u> and '<u>ready-to-eat</u>' it can be described as <u>high risk</u>.
5)   You can sometimes <u>identify</u> when a high risk food is <u>spoiling</u>
— e.g. meat going <u>slimy</u>, milk smelling <u>sour</u> or cheese going <u>mouldy</u>...
6)   ...but often <u>pathogenic bacteria</u> leave <u>no signs</u> — <u>taste</u>, <u>colour</u>, <u>odour</u> and <u>texture</u> aren't affected.
7)   You can check there are no <u>visible</u> signs of spoilage when <u>buying food</u>:
• <u>Fresh meat</u> should be brightly coloured, firm and have a fresh smell.
• <u>Fresh fish</u> should have shiny skin, red gills, clear eyes and smell clean or slightly salty.

Double, double, spoil and trouble...

Microorganisms, such as bacteria, multiply much more quickly in the right conditions.
Luckily, you're able to slow the rate at which they do so by changing one or more of the factors above. Phew.

Q1   Explain, for each choice below, which food bacteria would grow more quickly in:

a) Whole milk or powdered (dried) milk   [2 marks]

b) A refrigerated pizza or a pizza at room temperature   [2 marks]

Food Spoilage

Fruit and vegetables <u>change</u> over time — e.g. <u>unripe</u> blackberries are <u>green</u> and <u>turn black</u> when they are <u>ripe</u>. This is the work of <u>enzymes</u>...

Enzymes are Biological Catalysts

<u>Enzymes</u> are <u>special proteins</u> that act as <u>biological catalysts</u> — they <u>speed up</u> chemical <u>reactions</u>. You can see the <u>effects</u> of enzymes in many <u>fruits</u> and <u>vegetables</u>:

Ripening
- <u>Enzymes</u> in fruit cause them to <u>ripen</u>, which affects the <u>sweetness</u>, <u>colour</u> and <u>texture</u> of the fruit.
- E.g. <u>Unripe</u> bananas are <u>green</u> and <u>firm</u> — enzymes <u>break down</u> <u>starch</u> inside them which makes the banana <u>softer</u> and <u>sweeter</u>.

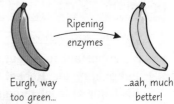

Ripening enzymes

Eurgh, way too green...   ...aah, much better!

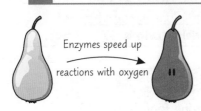

Enzymes speed up reactions with oxygen

Browning
- When you <u>slice</u> fruits (apples, pears etc.), the <u>oxygen</u> in the air will turn the fruit <u>brown</u>. Enzymes inside the fruit <u>speed up</u> this process.
- Leaving some fruit (bananas, avocados etc.) to <u>overripen</u> will give them a <u>brown colour</u> too.

These are examples of <u>enzymic browning</u>.

You can Slow or Stop an Enzyme from Working

You can have some <u>control</u> over the <u>activity</u> of enzymes — here are a few <u>methods</u> that will <u>slow</u> or <u>prevent</u> the <u>unwanted</u> effects of enzymes:

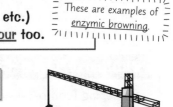

VAT O' LEMON

- <u>Adding an acid</u> — enzymes <u>work best</u> at a <u>certain pH</u>. If you dip slices of fruit into <u>lemon juice</u>, the acidic conditions will <u>stop enzymic browning</u>.

- <u>Blanching</u> (plunging into <u>boiling water</u> for a short period — see p.24) is used to <u>prepare</u> vegetables for <u>freezing</u>. Natural <u>ripening enzymes</u> will cause veg to lose <u>colour</u>, <u>texture</u>, <u>flavour</u> and <u>nutrients</u> over time. Freezing will <u>slow down</u> the enzymes but not stop them completely. Blanching <u>destroys</u> the ripening enzymes, so the vegetables <u>retain</u> their colour, nutrients etc.

Mould and Yeast Can Spoil Food Too

1) <u>Moulds</u> and <u>yeasts</u> are both <u>microorganisms</u> (<u>fungi</u>) — this means in the right conditions (<u>warmth</u>, <u>moisture</u> etc.) they can <u>grow</u> and <u>spread</u> quickly.
2) Moulds spoil <u>bread</u>, <u>cheese</u> and <u>fruit</u> — they can change the <u>look</u>, <u>smell</u> and <u>taste</u> of the food. You can easily spot mould due to its '<u>fuzzy</u>' appearance.
3) <u>Waste products</u> from moulds can cause <u>food poisoning</u> — even if you <u>scrape</u> it off, <u>toxins</u> may still remain.
4) <u>Yeasts</u> commonly grow on the surfaces of <u>fruit</u>, such as <u>grapes</u>, <u>blackberries</u> and <u>tomatoes</u>.
5) Yeasts can spoil fruit by <u>fermenting</u> the sugars, turning them into <u>alcohol</u> and <u>carbon dioxide</u>.

It was for a Science experiment, Mum! Honest!

Some moulds and yeasts are dangerous but many are useful for certain food products. See p.40 for more info.

A microorganism animated classic — 'Fruity and the Yeast'...

Enzymic browning is usually an unwanted effect but it is useful for things like tea — different types of tea can be made by controlling the amount of browning on the tea leaves. Neat.

Q1   Identify one sign of food spoilage that could affect a tomato.   [1 mark]

Q2   Explain how brushing banana slices with lime juice affects enzymic activity.   [3 marks]

Storing Food Safely

I like to eat food straight away — but some people out there like to <u>preserve</u> it. Where's the fun in that...

The Right Temperature is Vital to Storing Food Safely

To <u>preserve</u> food, you need to keep it in <u>conditions</u> that <u>bacteria can't grow</u> in.
First up, there are some <u>critical temperatures</u> that affect bacteria growth:

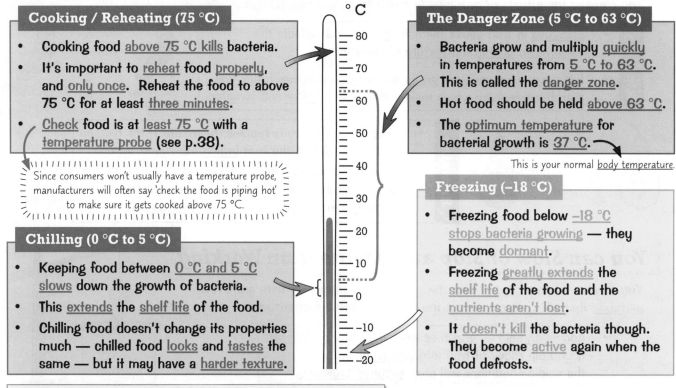

Cooking / Reheating (75 °C)

- Cooking food <u>above 75 °C kills</u> bacteria.
- It's important to <u>reheat</u> food <u>properly</u>, and <u>only once</u>. Reheat the food to above 75 °C for at least <u>three minutes</u>.
- <u>Check</u> food is at <u>least 75 °C</u> with a <u>temperature probe</u> (see p.38).

Since consumers won't usually have a temperature probe, manufacturers will often say 'check the food is piping hot' to make sure it gets cooked above 75 °C.

Chilling (0 °C to 5 °C)

- Keeping food between <u>0 °C and 5 °C</u> <u>slows</u> down the growth of bacteria.
- This <u>extends</u> the <u>shelf life</u> of the food.
- Chilling food doesn't change its properties much — chilled food <u>looks</u> and <u>tastes</u> the same — but it may have a <u>harder texture</u>.

The Danger Zone (5 °C to 63 °C)

- Bacteria grow and multiply <u>quickly</u> in temperatures from <u>5 °C to 63 °C</u>. This is called the <u>danger zone</u>.
- Hot food should be held <u>above 63 °C</u>.
- The <u>optimum temperature</u> for bacterial growth is <u>37 °C</u>.

This is your normal <u>body temperature</u>.

Freezing (–18 °C)

- Freezing food below <u>–18 °C</u> <u>stops bacteria growing</u> — they become <u>dormant</u>.
- Freezing <u>greatly extends</u> the <u>shelf life</u> of the food and the <u>nutrients aren't lost</u>.
- It <u>doesn't kill</u> the bacteria though. They become <u>active</u> again when the food defrosts.

Use a Fridge and Freezer Correctly

Fridges
1) Fridges should be <u>0 °C to 5 °C</u>, ideal for <u>chilling</u> foods (especially <u>high risk</u> foods).
2) Keep food <u>covered</u> or <u>stored in containers</u> to prevent <u>contaminating</u> other foods.
3) Don't let the <u>blood</u> and <u>juices</u> of raw meat <u>drip</u> onto other food — <u>always</u> store raw <u>meat</u>, <u>poultry</u> and <u>fish</u> on the <u>bottom shelf</u> in the fridge.

Freezers
1) Freezers are set at around <u>–18 °C</u>.
2) Food should have <u>clear labels</u> with the <u>date</u> they were frozen.
3) <u>Defrost</u> meat and poultry <u>thoroughly</u> in a <u>fridge</u> — if food is <u>partially frozen</u> the recommended <u>cooking time</u> may not be sufficient to <u>kill bacteria</u>...
4) ...or if <u>cooking from frozen</u>, follow the '<u>cook from frozen</u>' time.

You should also not overstock a fridge or freezer — air can't circulate so heat can't be removed efficiently.

<u>Freezers</u> and <u>frozen foods</u> use a <u>star rating</u> to indicate how long to <u>store</u> food:

Storing in an ice box / freezer compartment of a fridge:	Storing in a domestic freezer:
* 1 week (–6 °C)	*** 3 months (–18 °C)
** 1 month (–12 °C)	**** Until '**best before**' end date (–18 °C or colder)

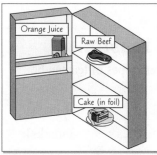

Orange Juice
Raw Beef
Cake (in foil)

Frying through the danger zone...

Temperature control is really important, so make sure you can recall all of the critical temperatures above. Now, take a look at this immaculately drawn fridge on the left...

Q1 Explain whether the food in the fridge has been stored correctly. [2 marks]

Q2 Sean cooks the beef and places the leftovers back in the fridge. Explain the benefit of refrigerating the cooked beef. [2 marks]

Storing Food Safely

Temperature control is vital for storing food but you still need to regularly check use by and best before dates.

Some Food Can be Kept at an Ambient Temperature

Lots of food has to be chilled or frozen to extend its shelf life, but this isn't necessary for most things that we buy from the supermarket.

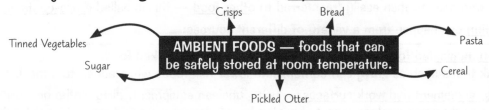

Crisps Bread

Tinned Vegetables

AMBIENT FOODS — foods that can be safely stored at room temperature.

Sugar

Pasta

Cereal

Pickled Otter

Stu's ambient soup was a little too tightly sealed.

1) Ambient foods should still be kept in a sealed container — keeping the air out keeps the food fresh.

2) They should be stored in a cool, dry place — any moisture will help the growth of moulds.

3) Ambient foods can be safe to eat after many months or years (e.g. dried pasta).

4) Methods of preservation are used to extend the shelf life of some foods:

- Freeze-drying — removes moisture from the food (e.g. instant coffee).

 • Canning foods — foods are sealed in cans and heated to kill off microorganisms.

 • Vacuum packing — food is put into plastic packaging, and the air is sucked out.

- Using chemicals — e.g. gherkins are pickled in vinegar, making it too acidic for microorganisms to grow quickly.

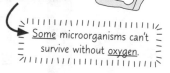

Some microorganisms can't survive without oxygen.

Don't Let Food go Past its Best

All food will eventually spoil or lose its quality — date marks must be printed on the packaging of the food you buy to help you know when the food is likely to be unsafe to eat or not taste as good.

Use By Date

- The 'use by' date is shown on products with a short shelf life, e.g. high risk foods.
- It's given as a safety warning. If you use the food after this date, it might not be safe — you run the risk of getting food poisoning.

Keep refrigerated

Cost	Use By
£ 2.50	24 JUN

Best Before Date

- The 'best before' date is shown on products with a longer shelf life, e.g. tinned foods.
- It's given as a warning about quality. If you eat the food after this date, it's probably safe but might not be as nice as you'd expect, e.g. biscuits could be soft.
- Eggs, however, are risky to eat after their best before date — salmonella bacteria (see p.39) may have multiplied to dangerous levels.

BEST BEFORE
08–02–17
Store in a cool, dry place.

Food might be OK a bit after its best before date, but it won't be fine forever.
A tin of baked beans from the 1960s is probably not going to be very nice on your toast.

Groovy Beans

GCSE revision — [Best Before: day of exam]...

There's a key difference between 'use by' and 'best before' dates — make sure you remember that 'use by' dates are about food safety and 'best before' dates are about food quality. Good. Let's crack on with some questions.

Q1 Give an example of an ambient food and describe a suitable method to store it. [3 marks]

Q2 Explain which type of date mark will be on the packaging of raw poultry in a supermarket. [2 marks]

Preparing Food Safely

If people eat food that's <u>contaminated</u> they could become very ill, so it's mega important that you handle food <u>safely</u> and <u>hygienically</u> to prevent bacteria spreading around the kitchen.

Avoid Cross-Contamination

When working with food, it's really easy to <u>pass bacteria</u> from <u>raw food</u> to <u>work surfaces</u>, <u>equipment</u> and your <u>hands</u>. Bacteria are then easily transferred to <u>other food</u> — this is called <u>cross-contamination</u>.

<u>Cross-contamination</u> can happen from a <u>variety</u> of <u>different sources</u>:

- <u>Other contaminated food</u> — raw meat juices can drip onto cooked food. High risk foods such as gravy can contaminate lower risk foods when added to a meal.
- <u>Utensils, equipment and work surfaces</u> — using unclean equipment, dirty cloths on work surfaces or the same work surface / chopping board for raw meat and ready-to-eat foods.
- <u>People</u> — poor personal hygiene (especially unclean hands) and sneezing or coughing.
- <u>Pests</u> — flies, rodents etc. contaminate food directly by walking over / eating it or by laying eggs and droppings on work surfaces. Waste bins will attract pests.

Follow Safety and Hygiene Procedures

You should take steps to <u>reduce</u> the <u>risks</u> when <u>preparing</u>, <u>cooking</u> and <u>serving</u> food:

Preparing
- Follow <u>personal hygiene procedures</u> — <u>wash your hands</u>, wear a clean <u>apron</u>, wear a <u>hat</u> or <u>hair net</u> to cover your hair, remove all <u>jewellery</u>, cover all <u>cuts</u>.
- <u>Separate</u> raw and cooked foods and use <u>coloured chopping boards</u> for different food groups, e.g. you could use red for <u>raw meat</u> and brown for <u>raw vegetables</u>.
- <u>Wash raw vegetables</u> thoroughly — even traces of <u>soil</u> contain bacteria.
- Use <u>clean equipment</u> and an <u>antibacterial spray</u> to <u>sanitise</u> work surfaces.
- <u>Defrost</u> frozen food <u>fully</u>, in the bottom of a <u>fridge</u> and away from other food.

Cooking
- Cook food at the <u>right temperatures</u> (see p.36) and for <u>the correct time</u>.
- Make sure food is <u>cooked all the way through</u> — e.g. cook <u>thicker</u> pieces of meat for <u>longer</u> than thin ones.
- Test the temperature <u>inside</u> food using a temperature <u>probe</u>.

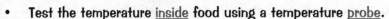
- <u>Sterilise</u> the probe <u>before</u> and <u>after</u> use.
- Insert it into the <u>middle</u> of the <u>thickest</u> part of the food.
- Leave the probe in until the temperature <u>stabilises</u>.
- Check that the probe reaches at <u>least 75 °C</u>.
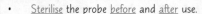

Serving

- Serve hot food <u>straight away</u> or keep it above <u>63 °C</u> for no longer than <u>2 hours</u>.
- If you're serving food <u>cold</u> or <u>storing</u> it, cool it down <u>within 90 minutes</u>.
- Keep food <u>covered</u> to prevent <u>flies</u> or other <u>pests</u> contaminating it — preferably put it in the <u>fridge</u>.
- Try to avoid <u>wasting food</u>, and check that waste bins are not <u>overfilled</u>.

I wouldn't cross with contamination if I were you...

It's dead easy for cross-contamination to happen. You have to be <u>very</u> careful and hygienic in the kitchen — especially if you're dealing with high risk foods that bacteria just lurrrveee.

Q1   Explain how each of the following is a food safety risk:

     a) Preparing all meals on one chopping board.   [2 marks]

     b) Allowing my pet cats Mylo and Ziggy on the kitchen work surfaces.   [2 marks]

Food Poisoning

Hope you're not eating your lunch... it's time to take a peek at the most common <u>types</u> of <u>bacteria</u> that cause <u>food poisoning</u> and their (rather unpleasant) <u>symptoms</u>.

Bacteria Can Cause Food Poisoning

1) The <u>general symptoms</u> of food poisoning include <u>sickness</u>, <u>diarrhoea</u>, <u>stomach cramps</u> and <u>fever</u>. In extreme cases, especially where people are <u>old</u>, <u>very young</u> or <u>vulnerable</u>, it can lead to <u>death</u>.

2) You can get food poisoning by eating <u>contaminated</u> food containing <u>pathogenic bacteria</u> — it can take a <u>few hours</u> to <u>several days</u> before you get any <u>symptoms</u>.

3) There are <u>many different</u> types of bacteria — you need to <u>learn</u> some of the <u>common</u> ones...

Remember these Main Types of Bacteria

Campylobacter

- The <u>most common</u> cause of <u>food poisoning</u> in the UK.
- Found mainly in <u>raw or undercooked poultry</u>, but also in other <u>raw meat</u>, and untreated <u>milk</u> / <u>water</u>.
- Onset time: 2–5 days.

> Onset time is the time it takes from ingesting the bacteria to when symptoms first appear.

> Who you calling a squid, punk?

E. coli O157

- E. coli live in the <u>intestines</u> of <u>animals</u>.
- Most types are <u>harmless</u> but <u>E. coli O157</u> can cause <u>kidney damage</u> and <u>death</u>.
- Sources include <u>raw beef</u>, untreated <u>milk</u> / <u>water</u>, unwashed <u>vegetables</u> and <u>salad leaves</u>.
- Onset time: 1–3 days.

Salmonella

- Found in <u>raw poultry</u>, untreated <u>milk</u> and <u>eggs</u>.
- Onset time: 6–72 hours.

Listeria

- <u>Listeria</u> can be found in <u>soft cheeses</u>, <u>pâté</u> and <u>shellfish</u>.
- <u>Unlike</u> other bacteria it can <u>grow</u> in <u>cold temperatures</u>, such as in a <u>refrigerator</u>.
- <u>Pregnant</u> women are at a <u>higher risk</u> of infection — and it can lead to <u>miscarriage</u> or <u>health problems</u> in the child.
- Onset time: Up to 70 days.

Staphylococcus aureus

- Found on the <u>skin</u>, <u>hair</u> and in the <u>noses</u> of <u>animals</u> and <u>people</u>.
- Onset time: 1–6 hours.

> 'S. aureus' ends in 'us' — so it's easy to remember that you can find it in humans.

Controlling Bacteria

Two <u>common foods</u> that could be contaminated with bacteria are <u>untreated milk</u> and <u>eggs</u>, so there are <u>methods</u> in place to make these foods <u>safe</u> for us to eat:

- <u>Pasteurisation</u> — all milk sold in supermarkets is <u>pasteurised</u>. Milk is <u>heated</u> at around <u>72 °C for 15 seconds</u> to kill off any <u>pathogenic</u> bacteria before being <u>chilled</u>.
- <u>Vaccinations</u> — the <u>British Lion Quality</u> mark on egg shells and boxes is for hens that have been vaccinated against <u>salmonella</u>, so that it doesn't contaminate their <u>eggs</u>.

I just can't stand salmonella, ella, ella...

There are some big, scary names for these bacteria — you'll need to learn how to <u>spell</u> them (it took me a good 10 minutes to spell ~~Staffylowcouscous~~ Staphylococcus aureus) and the <u>key facts</u> about each.

Q1   Explain how a chef can reduce the risk of salmonella when preparing a dish containing eggs.   [3 marks]

Uses of Microorganisms

The last page has probably left a <u>bad taste</u> in your mouth and you'll be forgiven for thinking that all microorganisms are bad for us... but hopefully this page will <u>convince</u> you that's <u>not the case</u>.

Moulds are Added to Blue Cheese

Some moulds are <u>safe</u> to eat — these moulds are really important in the <u>production</u> of <u>certain cheeses</u>.

- The blue bits on <u>blue cheese</u> (e.g. <u>Gorgonzola</u>, <u>Stilton</u>) are due to the <u>moulds</u> that have been <u>added</u> to them.
- The mould gives the cheese a <u>creamy texture</u> and a distinctive <u>sharp</u>, <u>tangy</u> taste.

Cheesy fact: blue cheeses have a strong smell — this is caused by the same bacteria behind foot and body odour. Lovely!

Yeasts are Used to Make Bread Rise

The production of many <u>varieties of bread</u> relies on the properties of <u>yeast</u> as a <u>raising agent</u> (p.32).

- <u>Yeast</u>, <u>flour</u> and <u>water</u> form a <u>dough</u>. <u>Salt</u> is added for <u>flavour</u>, but also to <u>strengthen</u> the <u>gluten</u> in the dough.
- With the <u>ideal conditions</u> (warmth, moisture etc.), the yeast quickly starts to <u>grow</u>.
- The yeast ferments the sugar to produce <u>carbon dioxide</u> — this gas is what causes the bread to <u>rise</u>.

<u>Sourdough bread</u> uses <u>naturally occurring</u> bacteria and yeast already in the flour, rather than adding commercial baker's yeast — this produces a distinctive, slightly sour taste.

Bacteria are Used to Make Yoghurt

<u>Non-pathogenic</u> bacteria don't make you <u>ill</u> and are oh-so-useful in turning <u>milk</u> into cheese and <u>yoghurt</u>.

- Milk is <u>pasteurised</u> to kill off any <u>'bad' bacteria</u>.
- <u>Non-pathogenic</u> bacteria are added.
- These bacteria <u>ferment lactose</u> (milk sugar) and produce <u>lactic acid</u>.
- The lactic acid acts on the proteins in the milk to <u>thicken</u> it and gives it a <u>sour</u> or <u>tangy</u> taste.
- <u>Probiotics</u> (live bacteria) are a <u>supplement</u> in some yoghurts which are <u>said</u> to give <u>health benefits</u>.

Told you so — some bacteria ne-ferment to hurt you...

There you have it — some marvellous uses of microorganisms. Once you're familiar with all three examples, give this question a whack, then head on over to the next page for some revision questions on this section.

Q1   Explain the role of microorganisms in the production of:

a) Baguettes   [2 marks]

b) Tzatziki (a Greek sauce made with yoghurt)   [3 marks]

Revision Questions for Section Three

I'm sorry once again if <u>section 3</u> put you off your lunch, but all that chat about bacteria is almost over... last thing to do is to tuck into these revision questions I've handpicked especially just for you.

- Try these questions and <u>tick off each one</u> when you <u>get it right</u>.
- When you've done <u>all the questions</u> for a topic and are <u>completely happy</u> with it, tick off the topic.

Food Spoilage (p.34-35) ☑

1) What is a pathogenic microorganism?
2) Which five conditions are needed for the growth of microorganisms?
3) What is a high risk food? List five types of food that would be classed as high risk.
4) How do ripening enzymes change the properties of fruit and vegetables?
5) Explain what enzymic browning is.
6) Rhea is preparing a fruit salad. She says she can preserve it using lemon juice. Explain how lemon juice would help her preserve the fruit salad.
7) How do yeasts spoil fruit?

Storing & Preparing Food Safely (p.36-38) ☑

8) Give the temperature, or range of temperatures, at which you would:
   a) reheat food   b) chill food   c) freeze food
9) What is meant by the danger zone?
10) How does freezing affect the shelf life of food?
11) What is the correct way of storing uncooked meat in a refrigerator?
12) What is an ambient food? Give an example.
13) How is a 'use by' date different from a 'best before' date?
14) What is 'cross-contamination'? List four possible sources of it.
15) Write a set of instructions to explain how to use a temperature probe correctly.
16) Delphine is making beef bourguignon — a stew prepared with braised beef. Give three safety steps she should take for each of these stages:
   a) preparing   b) cooking   c) serving the beef bourguignon

Food Poisoning (p.39) ☑

17) List four general symptoms of food poisoning.
18) For each type of bacteria, say where it can be found:
   a) Campylobacter
   b) E. coli
   c) Staphylococcus aureus
19) What is the 'onset time'? Which type of bacteria has an onset time of less than 6 hours?
20) Name two types of bacteria that could be found in raw minced beef.
21) Explain the process of milk pasteurisation.
22) How can you spot eggs from hens vaccinated against salmonella?

Uses of Microorganisms (p.40) ☑

23) What texture and taste do moulds give to blue cheeses?
24) How are microorganisms used in the production of:
   a) Bread
   b) Yoghurt?

Influences on Food Choice

There are loads of different things that affect your <u>food choices</u>.
Fortunately, this section will break them down into small, digestible, chocolate-coated chunks...

Many Factors Influence What People Choose to Eat

You need to learn these <u>10 factors</u> which influence people's food choices.

Physical Activity Level (PAL)

- Different people have different physical activity levels (PALs, see p.16).
People with higher PALs need <u>more calories</u>.

- A person who has an <u>active</u> lifestyle (e.g. someone who walks 3 or more miles a day) will need to consume around 20% more calories per day than someone with a <u>sedentary</u> (inactive) lifestyle.

- Sportsmen/sportswomen may choose food to help <u>improve</u> their <u>performance</u>, e.g. <u>high protein</u> foods to help build <u>muscle</u>, or high carb foods to help with <u>endurance</u>.

Healthy Eating

- People trying to eat <u>healthily</u> will choose foods based on their <u>nutritional</u> value, e.g. foods <u>low</u> in <u>sugar</u> and <u>fat</u>, and high in <u>vitamins</u> and other nutrients.

- People with <u>allergies</u> or <u>intolerances</u> will need to avoid certain foods.

Obligatory healthy veg pic

Cost of Food

- People choose food based on its <u>price</u>. Generally, they'll go for the <u>cheaper</u> option, unless they think it's worth paying more for <u>better quality</u> (see below).

- People will go for foods on <u>special offer</u> — everyone likes a bargain (see p.48).

- Supermarkets often show a <u>price per gram</u> to help people compare different products. Some people will buy food in <u>bulk</u> to get a lower price per gram.

- It can be <u>cheaper per portion</u> to <u>make</u> your own food than buy ready meals, but it'll usually cost more to buy the ingredients all at once than buy a single ready meal.

You should be able to cost your recipes. See p.19 for more information.

Income

- People on <u>high</u> incomes are more likely to buy <u>expensive</u> items, because a high price means (or at least suggests) it's of a higher <u>quality</u>.

- People on <u>low incomes</u> are more likely to go for the <u>cheaper</u> food option. Fresh meat, fruit and vegetables can be <u>pricey</u>, so it's more likely they'll opt for <u>cheaper</u>, <u>processed</u> foods (often high in fat and salt).

- In general, people on <u>lower</u> incomes tend to have <u>poorer</u> diets than high income groups.

Culinary Skills

- Some people are <u>great</u> cooks, some are more "<u>beans on toast</u>". Many people just lack the <u>confidence</u> to cook.

- People may not try <u>difficult-looking</u> recipes in case it all goes wrong or they just don't enjoy it. They may not want to risk <u>wasting</u> their money on ingredients, especially if a <u>ready-made</u> alternative is available.

Caution: Overconfidence may lead to loss of digits.

Influences on Food Choice

What, more? Learn as many of these <u>influences</u> as possible, and the <u>reasons</u> behind them.

Lifestyle

- People who are feeling <u>stressed</u> or <u>bored</u> are more likely to go for <u>comfort food</u> (generally <u>high</u> in <u>fat</u> or <u>sugar</u>).
- People leading <u>busy</u> lives, e.g. long working hours or time-consuming hobbies, can <u>struggle</u> to find time to make a proper meal. This can make it tempting to just grab unhealthy food 'on the go'.
- People have different eating <u>patterns</u> — some have proper meals at set times of day, others tend to 'graze' throughout the day.
- Some people have <u>bad habits</u> like eating very late just before bed (not good for digestion) or regularly <u>skipping breakfast</u> (probably the worst sin of all).

With Rita's dedication to weaving, she had no time to prepare meals.

Seasonality

- Certain UK grown foods are only available at <u>certain times</u> of year. For example, UK grown courgettes are available between June and September (see p.61).
- People worried about the environmental impact of <u>food miles</u> (p.61) may buy <u>local foods</u> that are in season and <u>avoid</u> imports from around the world.

Availability

- People are more likely to buy and eat foods which are readily <u>available</u>. E.g. people in <u>rural</u> areas may have to shop at a <u>small local store</u> with <u>limited</u> food options.
- However, with <u>online shopping</u> on the rise, more and more people in rural areas are able to order online and have the supermarkets <u>deliver to them</u>. Handy.

Special Occasions

- Special occasions are often <u>celebrated</u> with a <u>large meal</u>. E.g. Fattening meals such as <u>turkey roast</u> and <u>suet pudding</u> are served at Christmas time in the UK, but they are far less common at other times of year.

Enjoyment

- Unsurprisingly, people tend to choose the food that they <u>enjoy</u>.
- You might think that it's all about <u>flavour</u>, but <u>smell</u>, <u>appearance</u> and <u>texture</u> all affect a food's <u>palatability</u> (how appealing it is).
- One downside of eating what you enjoy is it's often not very healthy. Humans are generally drawn towards <u>sweet</u> or <u>fatty</u> foods.
- People generally aren't drawn towards <u>bitter</u> foods, although some bitter foods are hugely popular once you get the 'taste' for them, e.g. coffee, dark chocolate, beer...

When I click my fingers you'll crave mashed potato...

Some of these influences may seem obvious, some may surprise you. Regardless, learn them all then try this.

Q1   Explain how a low income can affect food choice and diet.   [2 marks]

Q2   Explain how working long shifts and high levels of stress can lead to weight gain.   [3 marks]

Cultural, Religious and Moral Food Choices

Many cultures and religions have their own customs around what they do and don't eat.
In some there are strict rules, in others it's more guidance.

Different Religions have Different Views on Food

Many religions have specific dietary laws that should be followed.

Christianity

1) There are no strict rules about foods in Christianity.

2) During Lent, Christians often choose to give up certain foods or drinks.

3) During various Christian celebrations, special foods are eaten.
E.g. Hot cross buns on Good Friday (to represent the crucifixion of Jesus),
and pancakes to mark the start of Lent (by using up excess ingredients).

Islam

1) The Qur'an states that meats eaten by Muslims must be halal — where
the lawful animal is slaughtered in a specific way whilst being blessed.

2) Muslims cannot eat pork, nor any product made from pork products,
such as gelatine. Muslims are also not allowed to drink alcohol.

3) During Ramadan (the ninth month of the lunar calendar),
Muslims fast between sunrise and sunset.

In the lunar calendar, each month has 29-30 days and Ramadan falls at a different time each year.

Fasting is when no food is eaten for a period of time.

Hinduism

1) Many Hindus are vegetarian, but some tend to avoid certain vegetables that are considered
harmful such as garlic, onion and mushrooms.

2) The Hindus that eat meat require that it be slaughtered using a quick, painless method called
Jhatka. In Hinduism cows are considered sacred, so Hindus are not allowed to eat beef.

Judaism

1) Jewish dietary laws (kashrut) state that their food must be kosher (meaning fit for consumption).

2) Kosher animals are ones which have split hooves and chew cud (such as cows and deer), plus
fish that have fins and scales (so no shellfish). These animals must be slaughtered using quick,
painless methods which allow the blood to drain afterwards, as blood is considered non-kosher.

3) Jews are not allowed to eat pig, rabbit, hare, camel and many other animals.

4) Dairy and meats must not be cooked together or eaten together as a mixture.

Sikhism

1) Baptised Sikhs are prohibited from eating meat which is ritually
slaughtered (such as halal or kosher meat)

2) Many Sikhs are vegetarians.

3) Sikhism teaches that its followers should only eat what
they need to, and should avoid overindulging.

For more on planning food for groups, see p.19-20.

Buddhism

1) Buddhists believe that all living beings are sacred, so the majority of Buddhists are vegetarian or
vegan (although there are no strict rules on this).

2) Most Buddhists avoid alcohol, as they believe it wrongly alters your view of the world around you.

3) Some Buddhists choose to fast from noon until sunrise the following day.

Rastafarianism

1) Eating pork is forbidden in Rastafarianism.

2) Many Rastafarians stick to an I-tal (clean and natural) diet, meaning the diets are mainly
made up of fresh vegetables. Some eat fish, but the fish must be less than 30 cm long.

3) Many Rastafarians do not drink alcohol but will drink things made from
natural, grown products, such as herbal tea or fruit juice.

Cultural, Religious and Moral Food Choices

There's more to <u>food choice</u> than just being <u>picky</u>. Some people choose their food based on <u>moral reasons</u>, whereas others must choose carefully to avoid getting <u>very ill</u>.

Food Choices Are Influenced by Moral or Ethical Concerns

'<u>Moral</u>' and '<u>ethical</u>' just mean 'what people think is <u>right or wrong</u>'. Loads of people choose food based on their idea of right and wrong, with reasons like the following:

Animal Welfare

Animal welfare is a concern for many people. People may choose to eat foods where they know the animals have been treated <u>ethically</u>, such as <u>free-range</u> products (p.57), or they may <u>avoid meat</u> altogether, e.g. <u>vegetarians</u>, <u>vegans</u> (p.20).

Working Conditions

- <u>Fairtrade</u> products, e.g. bananas, are popular with customers who want to make sure the farmers in developing countries get a <u>fair price</u> for their <u>produce</u> (see p.63).
- Fairtrade products are often slightly more <u>expensive</u> to buy than non-Fairtrade items.

Environmental Impact

- People may prefer to buy <u>British</u> or <u>local produce</u>, or foods that are in season, in order to support the local <u>economy</u> and to <u>reduce food miles</u> (see p.61).
- Some <u>fish</u> products say whether the fish were caught using <u>sustainable</u> fishing methods, to avoid damaging the ecosystem and stop fish from going extinct (see p.58).

Eating Naturally

- Some people prefer to eat <u>organic</u> foods (p.55) — ones that have been produced <u>without</u> the use of <u>synthetic chemicals</u>. Organic foods are grown using <u>natural fertilisers</u> and <u>natural pest control</u>.
- People may <u>avoid</u> buying genetically modified foods, over concerns about <u>unwanted effects</u> on the <u>consumer</u> and <u>environment</u> (p.56).

People with Intolerances or Allergies Must Avoid Certain Foods

1) Some people are <u>intolerant</u> to particular ingredients in food (p.20). Eating the food can lead to <u>illness</u>, and cause bloating, vomiting, pains etc.
2) Common intolerances are <u>lactose</u> (found in dairy products) and <u>gluten</u> (found in wheat, barley, oats and rye).
3) Food <u>allergies</u> may cause <u>serious illness</u> and can be <u>fatal</u> (p.20). Something that causes an allergic reaction is called an <u>allergen</u>.
4) The most common allergens are <u>nuts</u>, <u>eggs</u>, <u>dairy</u>, <u>wheat</u>, <u>fish</u> and <u>shellfish</u>.
5) It's important that food is <u>properly labelled</u> so that people with <u>allergies</u> know what they can safely eat.

X-Melon: Acropalypse, coming soon to a field near you...

Go back through the page and think up some moral/ethical arguments for the influences above, then try these.

Q1 Explain how people may choose their food to support trade in developing countries. [2 marks]

Q2 What dietary laws must Muslims follow? [2 marks]

Food Labelling

Food labels can help people make informed choices about what they eat. There are tonnes of rules about what must appear on food labels and unfortunately you'll have to learn them.

Food Label Info is Controlled by Different Regulations

1) Countries in the European Union (EU) must follow the rules in the Food Information for Consumers regulations (FIC), updated in 2014.

2) The UK currently follows the regulations set out by the EU:

   - Food labels must not be misleading, e.g. making claims that the food can cure illness.
   - They must be clear and easy to read.
   - Common allergens must be emphasised (e.g. highlighted, bolded) in the ingredients.

3) From December 2016 it is compulsory for nutritional information to appear on food labels (next page).

4) In the UK, the Food Standards Agency (FSA) is responsible for making sure that food manufacturers and businesses are following the regulations (correctly labelling foods, using safe, hygienic practices, etc.).

Labels Must Tell You Certain Information by Law

EU laws say that the labels on pre-packed food have to tell you all this stuff:

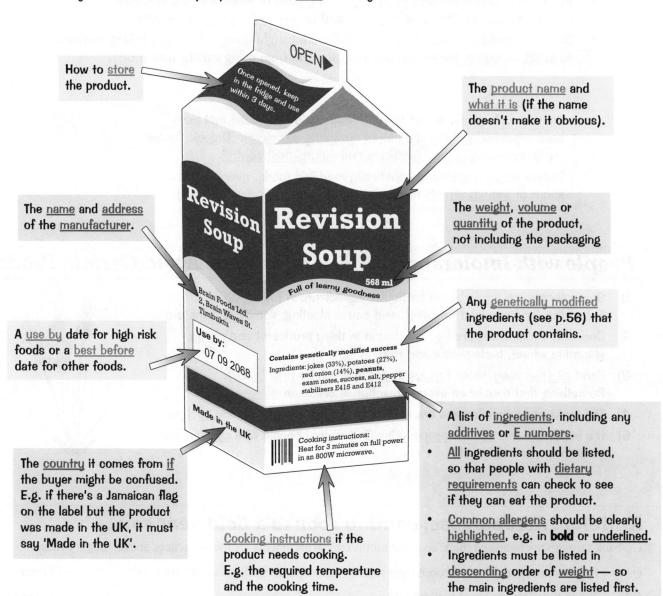

How to store the product.

Once opened, keep in the fridge and use within 3 days.

The product name and what it is (if the name doesn't make it obvious).

The name and address of the manufacturer.

Revision Soup

568 ml

Full of learny goodness

The weight, volume or quantity of the product, not including the packaging

Brain Foods Ltd. 2, Brain Waves St. Timbuktu

A use by date for high risk foods or a best before date for other foods.

Use by: 07 09 2068

Made in the UK

Contains genetically modified success
Ingredients: jokes (33%), potatoes (27%), red onion (14%), **peanuts**, exam notes, success, salt, pepper stabilisers E415 and E412

Any genetically modified ingredients (see p.56) that the product contains.

Cooking instructions: Heat for 3 minutes on full power in an 800W microwave.

The country it comes from if the buyer might be confused. E.g. if there's a Jamaican flag on the label but the product was made in the UK, it must say 'Made in the UK'.

Cooking instructions if the product needs cooking. E.g. the required temperature and the cooking time.

- A list of ingredients, including any additives or E numbers.
- All ingredients should be listed, so that people with dietary requirements can check to see if they can eat the product.
- Common allergens should be clearly highlighted, e.g. in **bold** or underlined.
- Ingredients must be listed in descending order of weight — so the main ingredients are listed first.

Food Labelling

Packaged food products should display certain <u>nutritional information</u>. This page will teach you <u>all about it</u>.

Nutritional Information Must Be Shown on Food Products

1) Since December 2016, manufacturers have had to include specific nutritional information on their packaging, although many have done this for years already.

2) Nutritional information should be shown in a table like this:

Energy is always given as kilojoules (kJ) and kilocalories, and the rest are given as grams.

NUTRITIONAL INFORMATION		
	per 100 g	per 55 g serving
Energy	2180 kJ/525 kcal	1199 kJ/289 kcal
Fat	33.0 g	18.2 g
of which saturates	15.0 g	8.3 g
Carbohydrate	50.0 g	27.5 g
of which sugars	2.0 g	1.1g
Protein	6.5 g	3.6 g
Salt	0.7 g	0.4 g

Each nutrient must be given per <u>100 g</u> of the food.

3) Other nutrient details <u>may</u> be listed, such as the amount of <u>fibre</u>, <u>vitamins</u> and <u>minerals</u>. This is not necessary, so it's up to the manufacturer to decide.

Labels Have Non-Compulsory Information on Them Too

Lots of other information that <u>doesn't have to be there</u> is often found on food packaging...

Product labels often make claims about the product in order to make the product look more <u>attractive</u> and <u>improve sales</u> (see next page). This is stuff like:

- <u>High in protein</u>
- <u>Low in fat</u>
- <u>Free</u> from <u>artificial colours</u> and <u>preservatives</u>

Food labelling rules are very strict and claims about health benefits must be truthful and accurate.

<u>Traffic-light labelling</u> on a product shows how <u>healthy</u> it is <u>at a glance</u>. They use Reference Intake values to show whether a product has <u>high</u>, <u>medium</u> or <u>low</u> amounts of fat, salt and sugar. For example, a <u>pizza</u> might be red for fat and yellow for salt and sugar.

per 54 g serving

Fat 2.4 g	Salt 0.2 g	Sugars 9.1 g
2%	4%	10%

% reference intake of an average adult

Products often state whether they are suitable for certain groups, e.g. <u>vegetarians</u>, <u>vegans</u>, <u>Muslims</u> (halal) and <u>coeliacs</u> (gluten-free) to make it <u>easier</u> for them to pick out the <u>correct</u> products.

Labels may say where the food / ingredients are <u>from</u> and where they were <u>packaged</u> or <u>processed</u>, e.g. 'Country of origin: Spain', 'Packaged in the UK'.

Labels may include <u>serving suggestions</u>, e.g. 'Try it with custard and a dollop of ketchup.'

CAUTION: Book may be hot whilst burning...

Make sure you know which things must legally be on the label, then give these questions a try. Such fun.

Q1 Calum is designing a label for his food product. So far, he's listed the ingredients.

    a) Why is it important that all of the ingredients are listed? [2 marks]

    b) State four pieces of information, other than the ingredients, that the label must include. [2 marks]

Q2 Explain two examples of non-compulsory information often given on food products. [2 marks]

Influences of Marketing

You find food adverts <u>everywhere</u> — from <u>TV ads</u> and <u>social media</u> to <u>magazines</u> and <u>posters</u>. There's more to marketing than just ads though. This page covers some of the <u>clever tricks</u> used to pull in customers.

Special Offers — the Oldest Trick in the Trolley

1) <u>Special offers</u> on food are a common sight in supermarkets.

2) Offers are used to <u>convince</u> customers to buy a product (or a quantity of it) that they wouldn't normally buy, by making it feel like they're getting a <u>bargain</u>.

> Examples of special offers are:
> - 'Buy one get one free' (BOGOF) or 'buy two, get the third free'
> - Reduced price (e.g. '30% off', or 'save £1.50')
> - Meal deals (e.g. main meal, dessert and a drink for £10)

BOGOF Mum!

Why you cheeky blighter.

3) <u>Loyalty card schemes</u> (where you get points for your shopping) allow supermarkets to record data about what you're buying, which they can use to send you offers <u>matched</u> to your <u>buying habits</u>.

4) <u>Point of sale marketing</u> is used near the till — <u>carefully chosen</u> items (chocolate, sweets, magazines, vouchers) are put on display in the hope that you'll <u>eventually</u> be tempted while you're queuing.

Celebrity or Brand Endorsement Can Increase Sales

1) Some companies use <u>endorsement</u> by <u>celebrity chefs</u> to <u>boost sales</u> — the chef's name is used to convince you that it's a quality product.

2) Food companies may partner up with big <u>film or TV brands</u> like 'Space Wars' — using 'Space Wars' on their products or adverts helps target certain <u>age groups</u>.

SPACE WARS
pasta shapes

May the sauce be ever in your flavour...

3) Food companies may <u>sponsor</u> sports and sportspersons, e.g. an energy drink company might sponsor a televised car rally. They'll <u>pay money</u> to put their name on advertising banners, cars, helmets, ... and benefit from it being seen by a <u>wide audience</u>.

Companies May Use Health Claims...

1) Food manufacturers may <u>promote</u> their food as having certain <u>health benefits</u> (e.g. high in vitamin C, 2 of your 5 a day). Claims that make a product appear <u>healthy</u> can <u>greatly increase sales</u>.

2) Manufacturers may also market a <u>low sugar</u> or <u>low fat</u> version of an <u>existing</u> product (e.g. diet cola), or one that only uses <u>natural</u> ingredients in order to attract buyers who are <u>health conscious</u>.

3) Special products such as <u>gluten-free</u> breads target customers who have specific dietary requirements.

...or Promote Their Ethical Values

1) Food companies may join ethical schemes like <u>Fairtrade</u> — it may cost them more to produce the food, but they can charge a <u>higher price</u> and the product will appeal to a <u>wider market</u>.

2) <u>Organic</u> food ranges may be produced to target certain groups — again, it'll cost more to produce, but the customers they're aiming at will probably be willing to pay a <u>higher price</u> for it.

3) Companies may advertise that they use <u>biodegradable</u> or <u>recycled materials</u> in their packaging, to attract customers concerned about the environment.

4) Product labels may use words like '<u>natural</u>' and '<u>fresh</u>' and use images of nature to make the product appear more natural (sometimes hiding the fact that they're actually full of artificial <u>chemicals</u>...).

You can go large for just 50p... *and have enough popcorn to feed a small country...*

Learn all of the sneaky marketing techniques on this page, then give these questions a try.

Q1 Give two ways an existing product can be tweaked in order to be sold as a healthy alternative. [2 marks]

Q2 Why may manufacturers use film franchises to promote their products? [2 marks]

British and International Cuisines

A <u>cuisine</u> is a style of cooking that is <u>representative</u> of a <u>particular country</u> or <u>region</u>. Different cuisines may have different <u>ingredients</u>, serving <u>styles</u> and <u>preparation</u> techniques.

Each Part of the UK Has Its Own Dishes

1) The United Kingdom has four countries — <u>England</u>, <u>Wales</u>, <u>Scotland</u> and <u>Northern Ireland</u>.
   Great Britain just consists of England, Wales and Scotland. Not a lot of people know that.

2) Traditional cooking techniques involve <u>stewing</u>, <u>roasting</u>, <u>baking</u>, <u>grilling</u>, <u>boiling</u> and <u>frying</u>.

3) Foods are baked or roasted in gas or electric <u>ovens</u>, or cooked in <u>pans</u> on stoves.

4) Meals are eaten <u>three</u> times a day — breakfast, lunch and dinner.
   Or breakfast, dinner 'n' tea if yer frum up North (like us).

5) Some traditional <u>ingredients</u> in UK cuisine are:

> <u>Meat</u>: Beef, lamb and pork — often made into sausages, ham and bacon.
>
> <u>Vegetables</u>: Potato, carrot, parsnips, cabbage, leek, onion, green beans, cauliflower.
>
> <u>Fish</u>: Haddock, eel, shellfish (such as crab, mussels, oysters), and mackerel.
>
> <u>Dairy and eggs</u>: Milk, cream, butter, cheese, chicken eggs.
>
> <u>Fruit</u>: Apples, pears, strawberries, blackberries, gooseberries, rhubarb, blackcurrants.

6) Here are some of the classic dishes each country is known for:

England

- <u>Cumberland sausage</u> — a coiled sausage flavoured with pepper and herbs.
- <u>Cottage pie</u> — beef mince, gravy and vegetables topped with grilled, mashed potato.
- <u>Cornish pasty</u> — pastry containing beef, potato, onion and swede.
- <u>Potted shrimps</u> — shrimps in melted butter.
- <u>Bread and butter pudding</u> — buttered bread soaked in milk, eggs, sugar and spices.
- <u>Fruit crumble</u> — stewed fruit topped with a crumbly biscuit or oat-based topping.

Northern Ireland

- <u>Crubeens</u> — boiled pigs' feet, which are battered and fried.
- <u>Irish stew</u> — casserole made with meat, potatoes, root vegetables and onions.
- <u>Soda bread</u> — bread made with bicarbonate of soda and buttermilk instead of yeast.
- <u>Potato farl</u> (Irish potato cakes) — a savoury Irish potato pancake.
- <u>Ulster fry</u> — a fried breakfast with soda bread, potato farls, bacon, sausage, egg and tomato.

Wales

- <u>Welsh rarebit</u> — toasted bread with a cheese sauce, often containing mustard, beer or wine.
- <u>Bara brith</u> — cake with dried fruit and spices.
- <u>Laverbread</u> — slow cooked seaweed paste.
- <u>Glamorgan sausage</u> — a vegetarian sausage made with cheese and leeks, and coated in breadcrumbs.
- <u>Welsh cakes</u> — small, round flat cakes with raisins baked on a griddle.

Scotland

- <u>Scotch broth</u> — soup made with red meat, root vegetables, barley and dried pulses.
- <u>Neeps and tatties</u> — swede and potatoes cooked in oil and mashed.
- <u>Haggis</u> — lamb (and sometimes beef), suet, onion, oatmeal, seasoning and spices.
- <u>Shortbread</u> — a buttery and crumbly biscuit made with butter, flour and sugar.

British Food is Often Served with Sauce and Vegetables

1) Hot meat dishes are often served with a <u>sauce</u>, e.g. roast beef with gravy.

2) Main courses usually pair <u>meat</u> or <u>fish</u> with potatoes and other vegetables.

3) Food is eaten with <u>utensils</u> — forks, knives and spoons.

4) Hot desserts, e.g. sticky toffee pudding and apple pie, may be served with <u>cream</u>, <u>ice cream</u> or <u>custard</u>.

5) Modern takes on traditional recipes include chilli con carne filled cottage pie topped with sweet potato, salted-caramel apple crumble, and a bread and butter pudding made with brioche and marmalade.

British and International Cuisines

Now we'll show you a <u>couple of examples</u> of <u>different cuisines</u>, and the <u>type of things</u> you'd need to know about them. If you've studied different cuisines, make sure you learn <u>all this and more</u> about them.

Traditional Japanese Meals Consist of Rice and Okazu

1) Japanese cuisine mainly consists of <u>steamed rice</u> (gohan), combined with a number of <u>okazu</u> (dishes to eat with rice).

2) <u>Boiling</u>, <u>steaming</u> and <u>frying</u> are all popular cooking techniques.

3) <u>Rice cookers</u> and <u>woks</u> are used regularly in Japanese cooking. Bamboo steamers are used for steaming things like dumplings.

4) <u>Three</u> meals are eaten each day — in the morning, at midday, and in the early evening (the largest meal of the day).

5) Common ingredients in Japanese cuisine are:

> <u>Rice:</u> Rice is eaten with nearly every meal. It is also used to make desserts and sweets.
> <u>Noodles:</u> Strands of dough that are stretched and cut into shapes.
> <u>Seafood:</u> Such as salmon, mackerel, tuna, squid. Served raw (sashimi) or grilled.
> <u>Saké/Mirin:</u> Japanese rice-wines. Mirin is sweeter than saké, and also has a lower alcohol content.
> <u>Pickled vegetables:</u> Vegetables preserved in vinegar. Served as an appetiser, side or topping.
> <u>Matcha tea:</u> Powdered green tea. Used in hot drinks and as flavouring in cakes, ice cream etc.
> <u>Wasabi:</u> A spicy horseradish-style paste.

6) Typical Japanese home-cooked dinners often have <u>one</u> course — in which multiple dishes are presented at once on separate plates or bowls.

7) Some traditional dishes in Japanese cuisine are:

<u>Sushi</u> — Sticky rice, often topped or rolled with raw fish (sashimi) and seaweed.

<u>Tempura</u> — Seafoods, vegetables or meat coated with batter and deep-fried.

<u>Gyoza</u> — Fried dumplings stuffed with meat or vegetables.

<u>Ramen</u> — Noodles in a soup, topped with vegetables, meat, eggs etc.

<u>Miso Soup</u> — a soup made from fermented soya beans, fungus and salt.

8) Desserts at the end of a meal are less common in Japan than in the UK. Sweet <u>rice cakes</u>, served with green matcha tea, are very popular. Red bean paste is a common filling in desserts.

Japanese Meals are Eaten with Chopsticks

1) <u>Chopsticks</u> are often used to pick up food, rather than using hands or cutlery. Rice and soup bowls may be held <u>close to the mouth</u> to make them easier to eat from, but plates should be left on the table.

2) People often <u>sit on floor mats</u> around low tables to eat.

3) Soup can be <u>slurped</u> from the bowl — it shows the chef that the food is being enjoyed.

4) Raw or pickled <u>ginger</u> is used to 'cleanse the palate', e.g. with sushi.

5) Modern twists on Japanese foods include <u>fusing</u> Japanese and <u>Western</u> dishes, e.g. BBQ pulled pork gyoza, matcha tea frappés, wasabi-flavoured chocolate, and using teriyaki (a Japanese sauce) on roast meats.

British and International Cuisines

Here's another <u>international cuisine</u> for you. Again, if you've been taught about two <u>different</u> international cuisines, make sure you know <u>this type of stuff</u> about them.

In Spanish Cuisine Lunch is the Largest Meal of the Day

1) In Spain three main meals are eaten throughout the day. Smaller eats may occur between main meals.

2) Typical cooking methods in Spain are stewing, charcoal grilling, plate grilling and cooking in a sauce.

3) <u>Breakfasts</u> are <u>small</u> and <u>light</u>, and are eaten first thing in the morning. People often break for a larger snack at around 10 am.

4) The <u>largest</u> meal of the day is <u>lunch</u> (2-4 pm), which often consists of 3 courses — a <u>starter</u>, <u>main</u>, and <u>dessert</u> and/or coffee. <u>Dinner</u> is a <u>lighter meal</u> eaten around 9-11 pm.

5) Typical ingredients in Spanish cuisine:

> <u>Meats</u>: Pork, chicken and seafood.
> <u>Herbs and spices</u>: Peppers, nutmeg, paprika, cumin and coriander.
> <u>Fruit and Veg</u>: Peppers, olives, garlic, tomatoes, oranges, lemons.
> <u>Other</u>: Almonds, olive oil, beans, wine.

6) Spain produces a huge amount of wine — it's often served with meals.

7) The Spanish lunch <u>usually</u> has three courses, but can have up to six: Appetiser, first course, fish dish, meat dish, dessert and coffee.

8) Examples of Spanish foods include:

<u>Churros</u>: thin strips or loops of fried dough, often dunked in hot chocolate or chocolate sauce.

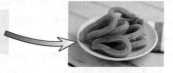

<u>Serrano ham</u>: a type of cured ham.

<u>Chorizo</u>: a spicy cured pork sausage.

<u>Paella</u>: a rice dish made in a large flat plan, made with stock, seafood (such as squid, shrimp and mussels), chicken or other meats, and vegetables. It is commonly cooked in huge portions for festivals.

<u>Patatas bravas</u>: spiced, fried potato chunks served with a spicy tomato sauce.

<u>Tapas</u>: Small savoury dishes eaten as a snack or like a buffet (where many dishes are shared between a group of people). Examples include: king prawns in garlic and chilli, patatas bravas (see above), chorizo (see above), grilled fish, fried squid, filled tortillas, Spanish omelette.

9) Traditional Spanish recipes have been <u>modernised</u> in many ways, such as using quinoa or noodles in paella, vegetarian paella and flavoured churros. Chorizo is often used in <u>non-Spanish</u> dishes like pasta or omelettes.

This is REALLY making me want a holiday to Tokyo or Barcelona...

You'll need to be able to write about all the stuff on these pages. If you've already learned about two other types of international cuisine, make sure that you can rhyme off the type of facts shown on these pages.

Q1   Describe three traditional British dishes, stating the country that they come from.   [3 marks]

Q2   Choose an international cuisine and a) list four ingredients commonly used in it.   [2 marks]
                                                b) describe three traditional dishes associated with it.   [3 marks]

Sensory Testing

What would you rather eat — a cupcake that smells like <u>old cheese</u> or a packet of <u>crunchy</u> roast-dinner flavoured <u>mealworms</u>? We use a combination of senses to try and figure out what we should eat.

Humans Taste by using their Tongue and Nose

1) Human tongues are covered in thousands of taste buds, which detect five different things — <u>salt</u>, <u>sweet</u>, <u>sour</u>, <u>bitter</u> and <u>umami</u> (savoury).

2) We use <u>taste buds</u> in conjunction with <u>olfactory receptors</u> in the nose (which detect <u>smells</u>) to identify the flavour of foods.

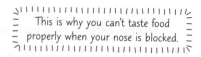
This is why you can't taste food properly when your nose is blocked.

Our Senses Influence Our Choice of Food

1) People use a combination of <u>senses</u> to decide whether a food is appetising.

2) Good food should appeal to the senses: <u>sight</u>, <u>smell</u>, <u>taste</u> and <u>touch</u>.

3) Each sense influences food choice in a different way:

Sight
We want food that <u>looks appealing</u>, e.g. that's colourful, looks fresh, is attractively presented... not a brown splodge on a plate.

Taste
Foods must have an enjoyable <u>taste</u>. The <u>method</u> of cooking, <u>freshness</u> of ingredients, choice of herbs, seasoning and flavour <u>combinations</u> all affect the overall taste.

Touch
Texture can make a surprising difference... We like our veg to be <u>crunchy</u> (not chewy and bendy), rice and pasta <u>firm</u> (not soggy), and 'wheat-biscuit' cereals with a little <u>crunch</u> (unless you're one of those strange people who leaves it to go soggy).

Smell
Smell helps us to <u>taste</u> food, and can also make us <u>want to</u> eat it (think of the smell of bread baking in the oven... or of chips... mmm). As above, how it's cooked and flavoured will affect the aromas that are given off.

Tests Are Used to Evaluate Food Products

Preference Tests Are Used to See Whether People Enjoy a Food

1) <u>Preference tests</u> are used to find out which <u>food</u> a person enjoys <u>more</u>.

2) Two popular types of preference test are the <u>paired preference test</u> and the <u>hedonic rating test</u>.

Paired Preference Test
1) In a <u>paired preference test</u> people are given <u>two slightly different</u> foods, e.g. two cookies — one made with butter and one made with margarine.

2) The taster chooses their <u>favourite</u> of the two foods.

Hedonic Rating Test
1) In a hedonic rating test people <u>rate</u> various foods using a <u>scale</u>, e.g. 1-5, Hate-Love.

2) The tasters are usually given a variety of different foods to rate.

Discrimination Tests Check if People Can Tell the Difference

1) One type of difference test is a <u>triangle</u> test — in this test, <u>three products</u> are <u>tasted</u>, where <u>two</u> products are the <u>same</u>, and one has a tweaked recipe. The taster must identify the one that <u>differs</u> from the others.

2) In an <u>A not A</u> test, <u>one</u> product is tasted first. The taster must then taste <u>two</u> more products, and identify which of the two is <u>identical</u> to the first one.

3) Triangle tests tend to give more <u>reliable</u> results than A not A tests, as there's less chance of <u>guessing</u> the right answer in triangle tests.

Sensory Testing

Behind many a great food product is a great <u>sensory test</u>. Sensory testing helps you understand what people really think of your product, so you can go away and improve it.

Grading Tests Are Used to Compare Food Characteristics

You need to know about three types of grading test, <u>ranking</u>, <u>rating</u> and <u>profiling</u>:

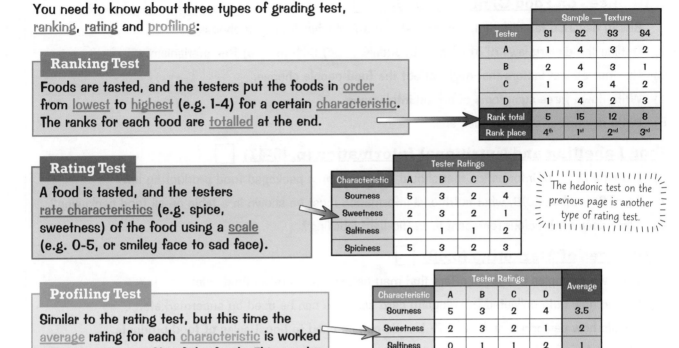

Ranking Test

Foods are tasted, and the testers put the foods in <u>order</u> from <u>lowest</u> to <u>highest</u> (e.g. 1-4) for a certain <u>characteristic</u>. The ranks for each food are <u>totalled</u> at the end.

Tester	Sample — Texture			
	S1	S2	S3	S4
A	1	4	3	2
B	2	4	3	1
C	1	3	4	2
D	1	4	2	3
Rank total	5	15	12	8
Rank place	4th	1st	2nd	3rd

Rating Test

A food is tasted, and the testers <u>rate characteristics</u> (e.g. spice, sweetness) of the food using a <u>scale</u> (e.g. 0-5, or smiley face to sad face).

Characteristic	Tester Ratings			
	A	B	C	D
Sourness	5	3	2	4
Sweetness	2	3	2	1
Saltiness	0	1	1	2
Spiciness	5	3	2	3

The hedonic test on the previous page is another type of rating test.

Profiling Test

Similar to the rating test, but this time the <u>average</u> rating for each <u>characteristic</u> is worked out to create a <u>profile</u> of the food. This can be displayed visually, e.g. on a star diagram.

Characteristic	Tester Ratings				Average
	A	B	C	D	
Sourness	5	3	2	4	3.5
Sweetness	2	3	2	1	2
Saltiness	0	1	1	2	1
Spiciness	5	3	2	3	3.25

Overlapping two star diagrams lets you easily compare two different foods at a glance, e.g. here, food A is rated more sour, but less sweet and salty than food B.

Key:
Food A
Food B

Food Tests Should Be Fair and Unbiased

1) You should make sure that you have chosen <u>enough</u> tasters for your panel (e.g. 10).

2) Tasters should <u>not be told</u> what each sample is — this is known as a '<u>blind test</u>'.

3) Tasters should work on their <u>own</u>, so they cannot be <u>influenced</u> by others.

4) Tasters should be given <u>clear instructions</u> on what they <u>need to do</u>.

5) Only <u>small samples</u> should be given to the tasters, to stop them filling up before the final samples.

6) Tasters should be allowed to drink <u>water</u> between samples to <u>wash the taste away</u>.

7) The tests should be carried out in:

- <u>Clean</u>, <u>hygienic</u> conditions.
- A <u>quiet</u> area.
- Similar testing areas with the same lighting, so that the food <u>looks</u> the <u>same</u> for each tester.

8) When testing is finished, manufacturers may use the results to make changes and improve their products.

And in first place... the runner beans...

If you're doing a sensory test, you need to make sure that you're not influencing the testers' decisions.
Go through everything on these pages, then cover them up and write down as much as you can.

Q1   Create a table for a rating test where four people test characteristics of a new scone recipe.   [2 marks]

Q2   Write down three rules that must be followed in a fair food test.   [3 marks]

Revision Questions for Section Four

Another day, another section. By now you should be a pro when it comes to understanding food choices, so:

- Try these questions and <u>tick off each one</u> when you <u>get it right</u>.
- When you've done <u>all the questions</u> for a topic and are <u>completely happy</u> with it, tick off the topic.

Influences on Food Choice (p.42-45) ☑

1) Briefly describe ten different factors that can affect what food you choose. ☑
2) Outline the dietary laws of a) Islam   b) Judaism   c) Sikhism   d) Rastafarianism. ☑
3) List four ethical factors that might affect the food people choose. ☑
4) Write down three symptoms of a food intolerance. ☑
5) Write down four common allergens. ☑

Food Labelling and Nutritional Information (p.46-47) ☑

6) List nine items of information that should be shown on a packaged food product by law. ☑
7) As of December 2016, what nutritional information must be shown in a table on all food packaging? ☑
8) What does each colour represent in traffic-light labelling? ☑

Influences of Marketing (p.48) ☑

9) Give two examples of special offers that may be used to increase food sales. ☑
10) Explain how data collected from loyalty card schemes can be used by supermarkets. ☑
11) Explain how celebrities and film / TV brands can be used to boost sales of food products. ☑
12) Why might a food company choose to sponsor a sporting event? ☑
13) How could a manufacturer modify an existing product to attract:
    a) health conscious customers
    b) customers worried about the environment? ☑

British and International Cuisines (p.49-51) ☑

14) For British cuisine:
    a) Describe the equipment / cooking methods used.
    b) Describe the eating patterns, e.g. when and how we eat.
    c) Describe five traditional foods or dishes.
    d) Describe two modern twists on traditional dishes. ☑

15) For Japanese and Spanish cuisines (or two of your choice):
    a) Describe the equipment / cooking methods used.
    b) Describe the eating patterns, e.g. when and how they eat.
    c) Describe five traditional foods or dishes.
    d) Describe two modern twists on traditional dishes. ☑

Sensory Testing (p.52-53) ☑

16) What are the five basic tastes? ☑
17) Explain the difference between paired preference and hedonic rating tests. ☑
18) Explain how the triangle discrimination test works. ☑
19) Outline the difference between ranking, rating and profiling tests. ☑
20) List four rules that should be followed to make sure food tests are fair. ☑

Grown Food

Food provenance is all about where your food <u>originally comes from</u> — it can be <u>grown</u>, <u>reared</u> or <u>caught</u>.

Crops are Grown Intensively or Organically

<u>Grown food</u> includes <u>fruits</u>, <u>vegetables</u> and <u>cereals</u>, e.g. wheat, rice, barley, oats, rye. There are two methods of farming them which you need to know about — <u>intensive farming</u> and <u>organic farming</u>.

Intensive Farming Uses Chemicals to Achieve Maximum Yields

<u>Intensive farming</u> uses methods that will produce the <u>highest possible yield</u> (more food from the same area of land). Production is often <u>large-scale</u>, with huge areas all growing the <u>same</u> crop.

1) <u>Large mechanical equipment</u> is used to <u>save time</u> and <u>cut down</u> on <u>production costs</u>.

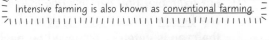
Intensive farming is also known as <u>conventional farming</u>.

2) <u>Artificial (chemical) fertilisers</u> are added to the soil to <u>supply nutrients</u> for crops to grow.

3) <u>Pesticides</u> are used. These are <u>chemicals</u> that <u>control pests</u> and <u>protect</u> crops and include <u>insecticides</u>, <u>herbicides</u> (<u>weedkiller</u>) and <u>fungicides</u>.

Get outta my grub!

4) Some people are <u>concerned</u> about using artificial <u>fertilisers</u> and <u>pesticides</u>. They can harm <u>wildlife</u>, damage the environment, e.g. by <u>polluting rivers</u>, and some think they have a harmful effect on <u>human health</u> too.

Organic Farming Uses Natural Methods

Organic food is grown naturally <u>without</u> using artificial fertilisers and pesticides. This makes it more <u>expensive</u> to produce.

1) Farmers add <u>organic matter</u> like <u>manure</u> and <u>compost</u> instead of artificial fertilisers.

2) Techniques such as <u>crop rotation</u> (growing different crops) and leaving land <u>fallow</u> (growing nothing) are used to make sure the soil is <u>fertile</u> every <u>year</u>.

3) Some farmers may use <u>alternative methods</u> to control pests. Things like:

- Introducing a pest's <u>natural predators</u> (e.g. ladybirds to eat aphids).
- <u>Biological pesticides</u> (e.g. certain fungi).
- Spraying crops with <u>hot water</u>.

4) These alternatives are generally <u>better</u> for the <u>environment</u>, but can be <u>more expensive</u> and <u>less effective</u> than using chemical pesticides.

5) Organic farming has its share of <u>advantages</u> and <u>disadvantages</u>:

Advantages	Disadvantages
• It <u>reduces</u> the amount of <u>chemical pesticides</u> going onto the land, so it's <u>less harmful</u> to the <u>environment</u>. • Fewer <u>non-renewable resources</u> are used than in intensive farming, so it's more <u>sustainable</u>. • It <u>appeals</u> to <u>consumers</u> (see p.45) who are <u>concerned</u> about the use of artificial <u>chemicals</u> and their damage to the <u>environment</u>.	• Organic farming tends to produce a <u>lower yield</u>. • There are higher <u>production costs</u>, which mean <u>higher prices</u> in <u>supermarkets</u>.

Intensive farming is a load of crop...

There are advantages and disadvantages for both intensive and organic farming — you should be able to discuss how crop yields, production costs and environmental impact differ between these two farming methods.

Q1   Describe the methods used in intensive farming and the environmental impact they have.   [3 marks]

Grown Food — GM Crops

People today are very concerned about <u>how</u> their food is <u>produced</u> and what <u>effect</u> it has on the <u>environment</u>. <u>Organic foods</u> are very popular, while lots of people are wary of <u>GM foods</u>.

Genetically Modified Foods Have Altered Genes

1) A genetically modified (<u>GM</u>) food is one that's had its <u>genes altered</u> to give it <u>useful characteristics</u>, such as improving its <u>growth</u> or changing its <u>colour</u>:

   - GM plants are produced by inserting a <u>desirable gene</u> from another plant, an animal or a bacterium into the plant you want to <u>improve</u>.
   - You plant modified <u>seeds</u> and up comes your GM crop.

2) For example, you can get GM maize that's <u>pest-resistant</u>. The <u>farmer</u> gets a <u>bigger yield</u> of maize because less of the crop is eaten or damaged by pests.

3) GM <u>weedkiller-resistant</u> crops can withstand chemicals that kill the <u>weeds</u> around the crop.

4) Currently, <u>no GM crops</u> are grown in the <u>UK</u>, but it's <u>popular</u> in other countries, e.g. the <u>USA</u> grows lots of GM <u>maize</u>, <u>cotton</u> and <u>soya beans</u>.

5) GM foods have both <u>advantages</u> and <u>disadvantages</u>:

Advantages

1) Crops can be made to <u>grow quicker</u>.

2) Producers can get <u>higher yields</u> of crops for the same amount of seed and fertiliser.

3) This makes food <u>cheaper</u> to <u>produce</u> so it's also <u>cheaper</u> for the <u>consumer</u> to buy.

4) Crops can be altered to have a <u>longer shelf life</u> — so less food is <u>wasted</u>.

5) Crops can be made to <u>ripen</u> earlier than normal, so <u>fresh foods</u> can be available for consumers <u>earlier</u> in the year.

6) Crops can be modified to contain <u>extra nutrients</u> which can improve <u>nutrition</u> in <u>poor countries</u>. E.g. <u>golden rice</u> has been genetically modified to contain carotene (which provides vitamin A).

Disadvantages

1) GM foods haven't been around for long — so their <u>long-term health effects</u> <u>aren't known</u>.

2) There are concerns that modified genes could get out into the wider <u>environment</u> and cause problems, e.g. the <u>weedkiller-resistance</u> gene could be transferred to a weed, making it an indestructible '<u>superweed</u>'.

3) GM producers can't sell their food everywhere — the <u>European Union</u> (EU) <u>restricts</u> the <u>import</u> of some GM foods.

Consumers Have Safety Concerns

1) Some people believe that we shouldn't <u>mess about with genes</u> because it's <u>not natural</u>.

2) In the European Union:

   - All GM foods must undergo <u>strict safety assessments</u> and can only be sold if no health risks have been identified.
   - All foods that are GM or contain more than <u>1% GM ingredients</u> must be <u>clearly labelled</u>.
   - However, meat and dairy <u>products</u> from animals fed on <u>GM feed</u> are <u>not labelled</u>.

Gene E — altered to give farmers three wishes...

No, you can't wish for more wishes — that's not allowed. Genetic modification is a fairly new technology which can help food producers and consumers — but not everyone is convinced that the benefits outweigh the risks.

Q1   Give a reason why a crop might be genetically modified.   [1 mark]

Q2   Give two reasons why some people are against GM products.   [2 marks]

Reared Food

Reared animals are animals raised by humans specifically for their meat (and other products).
E.g. cows are reared for beef and milk, and poultry (birds) for meat and eggs.

Factory-Farmed Animals Don't Have Much Space

Factory-farmed animals don't have much room to move — they may be in cages with lots
of other animals in the same place. This is another form of intensive farming.

1) Animals are kept inside in warm sheds, so they don't waste much energy moving or keeping
themselves warm. That means that more of their energy goes into producing meat or eggs for food
— this maximises food production.

2) Animals are sometimes given things like growth hormones or are
force-fed to speed up their growth — making it even quicker and
cheaper to produce meat.

3) Factory-farmed food is generally cheaper than free-range (see below)
— it's a more efficient way of farming, though it isn't as ethical.

4) People are becoming more concerned that intensively reared animals
don't live very nice lives — they're more likely to suffer from nasty
diseases, they can't behave naturally and are killed at a young age.

Factory farmed 'broiler' chickens might
be slaughtered after only 6 weeks.

5) Some people believe that meat from factory-farmed animals
doesn't taste as nice as meat from free-range animals.

6) Battery cages for hens were banned throughout the EU in 2012. New 'enriched cages' provide
slightly more space and nesting areas, but some people still argue that standards could be better.

Free-Range Animals Have More Space

Concerns for how reared animals are kept has led to an increase in people buying free-range food.

1) Free-range food (e.g. eggs) comes from animals that have more space
to live than factory-farmed animals — they're often free to roam.

2) Free-range animals have different amounts of space depending on the
brand you buy and aren't given hormones to speed up their growth.

3) They usually have nicer lives because of the higher standard of welfare.

4) Less food can be produced by rearing animals in free-range conditions — they use up
energy moving around, so take longer to grow. The extra land needed also adds to the cost.
This makes products more expensive and they might be beyond some people's budget.

5) Labels are added to foods to show they meet welfare standards. For example:

- The Red Tractor symbol on products lets consumers know that the
producer meets standards of food safety, hygiene, animal welfare and
environmental protection set by the Assured Food Standards scheme.
Farm assured food can be traced back to the farms they came from.

- The RSPCA Assured symbol can be found on eggs, fish and meat — to
get the logo, producers have to follow strict RSPCA welfare standards.
These standards cover every part of an animal's life, including
diet, lighting, bedding and how they're transported.

I had this reared dream once — I was being raised by a chicken...

More ethical products are generally more expensive — you'll need to be able to explain the reasons why.
If only there were a few questions to help with that...

Q1   What is meant by free-range food?   [1 mark]

Q2   Give two reasons why free-range foods are often more expensive than factory-farmed foods.   [2 marks]

Caught Food

Fish are a super source of <u>protein</u> and really benefit the <u>human diet</u>. Sadly, some fish species are so <u>popular</u>, like <u>North Sea cod</u>, that they have almost <u>disappeared</u> from our seas due to <u>overfishing</u>.

There are Different Fishing Methods

Fish can be <u>caught</u> or <u>reared</u> — the fishing method used depends on the <u>type</u> of fish and where it's <u>found</u>.

Trawling
- <u>Trawling</u> is a very common method of <u>fishing</u> — <u>trawlers</u> are fishing boats that catch fish using <u>nets</u>. Large trawlers may process fish on-board (<u>factory trawlers</u>).
- There are <u>different methods</u> of trawling — some <u>drag</u> a net through the <u>open sea</u>, and others along the <u>surface</u> of the <u>seabed</u> (bottom trawling).
- <u>Dredging</u> is like bottom trawling but uses a <u>metal 'basket'</u> instead of a net.

Fish Farming
- Large numbers of fish are <u>raised</u> in <u>tanks</u> or <u>enclosures</u> in rivers and lakes or in <u>cages</u> in the <u>sea</u>. E.g. <u>salmon</u>, <u>carp</u> and <u>trout</u>.
- As with <u>factory-farmed</u> land animals, there is <u>overcrowding</u> — the fish are more likely to suffer from <u>diseases</u>.

When the fish are <u>caught</u> they may be <u>washed</u> and <u>gutted</u> on the boats before they are brought to shore. Fish are <u>chilled</u> (packed with ice) or <u>salted</u> to prevent <u>spoilage</u> on the way to supermarkets and fishmongers.

Sustainable Fishing Preserves Future Fish Stocks

There is concern over how fishing methods are <u>damaging</u> the <u>environment</u>...

Bottom trawling is <u>destructive</u>, e.g. the nets that drag across the seabed can <u>destroy corals</u>, which are a <u>habitat</u> for lots of <u>marine life</u>.

Trawlers can also catch <u>unwanted</u> animals, like <u>dolphins</u> or <u>turtles</u>, in their nets.

<u>Overfishing</u> is when <u>more fish</u> are <u>caught</u> than can be <u>replaced</u> by natural reproduction. E.g. the demand for <u>bluefin tuna</u> to make <u>sushi</u> has led to overfishing. Bluefin tuna are now endangered (at risk of going <u>extinct</u>).

...so there needs to be <u>methods</u> to <u>conserve</u> fish stocks and make fishing more <u>sustainable</u>.

Alternative fishing methods
E.g. <u>Longline</u> fishing uses a fishing line with <u>baited hooks</u> secured between two buoys. <u>Fewer</u> fish are caught and there is less chance of catching <u>unwanted</u> fish.

A sustainable method is one that doesn't damage the environment or use up finite resources.

Fishing quotas
<u>Quotas</u> set by <u>governments</u> help <u>endangered</u> species of fish. They limit the <u>amount</u> and <u>sizes</u> of fish that can be caught.

Not falling for that again...

Regulating net size
Holes in fishing <u>nets</u> have to be a certain <u>size</u>, so that <u>smaller</u>, <u>unwanted</u> fish can escape.

Free krill! Today only.

Sustainable fishing — we cod do batter...

Learn the various fishing methods and how fishing can be made sustainable. Splendid! I'm off to the chippy.

Q1   Explain why bottom trawling is not considered a sustainable fishing technique. [3 marks]

Waste Food and Packaging

Millions of tonnes of food are thrown away each year — most of which could have been avoided.
Households, food producers and retailers all contribute to food wastage.

We Throw Away Lots of Food at Home

Households are big culprits when it comes to wasting food —
fruits, vegetables and bread are all thrown out unnecessarily.

REASONS FOR WASTING FOOD

1) Food has spoiled because:
   - It was overcooked or burnt
   - It wasn't covered or stored correctly
   - It wasn't kept at the right temperature
   - It had passed its use by date
2) Confusion over best before dates and
   other date marks — people wrongly think
   the food is no longer edible.

3) Too much food was cooked, and edible
   leftovers aren't frozen or reused.
4) Preparing food incorrectly —
   e.g. peeling vegetables too thickly.

Producers and Retailers Waste Food Too

A lot of food is wasted during production and by shops.

REASONS FOR WASTING FOOD

1) Retailers will reject food from producers if it is damaged or spoiled during transport.
2) Imperfect food (e.g. 'ugly' looking fruit) is often rejected by retailers too —
   the producer can't sell it, so it gets wasted.
3) To avoid running out of stock and disappointing their customers, supermarkets stock more than
   they can sell. The unsold stock gets binned, including stuff that is still safe to eat, like bread.
4) Offers from supermarkets encourage people to buy more than they can use or store.
5) Larger packs of food are better value for money — but again, it's often more than people need.

How We Can Reduce Waste

1) Plan meals and correct portion sizes — only buy ingredients that you will use.
2) Correctly store food and pay attention to use by dates.
3) Use up contents of your fridge before buying more food.
4) Use leftovers in meals the day after or freeze them for another time.
5) Use the whole food (e.g. bones can be used for stocks,
   peelings can be made into compost).
6) Donate unwanted food (cereals, pasta, beans etc.) to food banks.
   Some supermarkets are reducing their waste by donating unsold food.

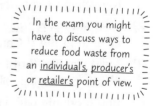

In the exam you might
have to discuss ways to
reduce food waste from
an individual's, producer's
or retailer's point of view.

XL double bacon cheeseburger — good waist food...

Food waste costs the average household around £500 a year, so it's a good idea to plan out your meals properly.
Not only that, but rotting food and packaging impacts the environment too — more about that on the next page.

Q1   Simon is planning to make some spaghetti Bolognese.
     Give some advice on how he could reduce food waste when preparing and cooking the meal.   [3 marks]

Q2   A supermarket has a 'buy one get one free' offer on cooked ham.
     Explain how this offer could have a negative impact on food waste.   [2 marks]

Waste Food and Packaging

Packaging is <u>pretty useful</u>, but like <u>waste food</u>, if it's <u>thrown away</u> it can damage the <u>environment</u>. Boo.

Packaging Protects and Preserves Food

Lots of different <u>materials</u> are used to <u>package food</u>.

- <u>Plastic</u> (cling film, vacuum-pack bags) — <u>transparent</u>, <u>lightweight</u> and can be <u>shaped</u> to the food.
- <u>Glass</u> (milk bottles, jars) — <u>transparent</u>, <u>heat-resistant</u>, gives food a <u>long shelf life</u> and is <u>reusable</u>.
- <u>Metal</u> (tins) — <u>heat-resistant</u> and gives food a <u>long shelf life</u>.
- <u>Paper</u> (pizza boxes, egg cartons, labels) — <u>lightweight</u>, can be <u>printed on</u> and is <u>biodegradable</u>.

Choosing <u>suitable</u> packaging <u>reduces waste food</u> because it:

- <u>Protects</u> food from being <u>damaged</u> while it's being <u>transported</u>, <u>displayed</u> and <u>stored</u>.
- <u>Preserves</u> the food and stops <u>contamination</u> from <u>bacteria</u> or <u>pests</u>.

Packaging also shows <u>useful information</u> to help customers (see p.46).

Packaging Can Be Bad for the Environment

<u>Excess</u> packaging is often used to make a product look more <u>appealing</u> to get a customer to buy it. But this <u>comes at a cost</u>...

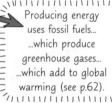

Producing energy uses fossil fuels... ...which produce greenhouse gases... ...which add to global warming (see p.62).

1) <u>Manufacturing</u> the materials for packaging uses lots of <u>energy</u> and <u>natural resources</u> — some of which are <u>non-renewable</u> (e.g. <u>plastics</u> from <u>crude oil</u>).

2) Packaging often gets used <u>once</u>, <u>thrown away</u> and then just takes up space in Britain's already huge <u>landfill sites</u>.

3) Some packaging, like <u>plastics</u>, take a long time to <u>biodegrade</u> (decompose), and could <u>take up space</u> in a landfill site for decades.

4) Packaging adds to the <u>weight</u> of a product, so heavier materials, such as <u>metals</u> and <u>glass</u>, require more energy to <u>transport</u> them.

5) <u>Litter</u> is <u>hazardous</u> to animals too — e.g. <u>marine life</u> can get <u>entangled</u> in <u>plastics</u> or <u>eat it</u> by mistake.

You Can Reduce the Environmental Impact

1) <u>Recycling</u> uses much <u>less energy</u> than manufacturing <u>new</u> packaging...

2) ...so always <u>recycle tins</u>, <u>glass</u>, <u>card</u> and <u>paper</u> — there are recycling <u>banks</u> all around the UK and local <u>councils</u> provide <u>recycling bins / bags</u> for homes.

3) Most <u>plastics</u> (bottles, pots, tubs and trays) can be recycled too. If in doubt, the <u>labels</u> on plastic packaging will tell you which <u>materials</u> are used and <u>whether</u> you can <u>recycle</u> them.

4) Buy products with little or no packaging and <u>refuse</u> ones with <u>excess packaging</u>.

5) Choose products with <u>biodegradable packaging</u> or packaging <u>made</u> from <u>recycled materials</u>.

6) Carry food in <u>reusable shopping bags</u> to reduce the need for <u>plastic bags</u>.

Since October 2015, large shops in England have to charge 5p for a plastic bag to encourage customers to re-use them instead.

Suspicious packaging — don't leave bags unattended...

So excess packaging is bad, but packaging still has an important job to do. Without it, foods would spoil and get damaged during transport, causing food waste. It's all about using the right materials... but not too much of them...

Q1   Give three ways that food packaging can have a negative impact on the environment.   [3 marks]

Food Miles and Carbon Footprint

Your food doesn't just magically appear in a <u>supermarket</u> — some of it's travelled <u>thousands of miles</u>.

Food Comes from Different Countries

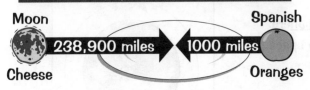

Food Miles — the distance food travels from where it's produced to the consumer.

Moon — 238,900 miles — Cheese

Spanish — 1000 miles — Oranges

1) Some food is <u>transported a long way</u> to be sold, e.g. some <u>green beans</u> you buy in the UK have come from Kenya.

2) This is bad for the <u>environment</u> — planes, ships and trucks all burn scarce <u>fossil fuels</u> and release <u>carbon dioxide</u> into the atmosphere, contributing to <u>global warming</u>.

3) But consumers now expect food to be <u>available all year round</u>, not just when it's in season here. So shops and manufacturers buy food from <u>abroad</u> when it's out of season at home, e.g. asparagus has a very short season here. Also, some things <u>just can't be grown</u> here, like bananas.

4) Manufacturing costs are <u>different</u> in other countries, so <u>imported food</u> can sometimes be <u>cheap</u>.

Buy Local Food to Reduce Food Miles

1) <u>Local food</u> is often better for the <u>environment</u> as it has few <u>food miles</u>.

2) Local food is often <u>fresher</u> and <u>tastier</u> because it reaches you soon after it has been harvested.

3) Buying from <u>farmers' markets</u> and independent <u>greengrocers</u> etc. <u>supports local businesses</u> and their produce can be <u>cheap</u>.

4) <u>Check labels</u> on foods from <u>supermarkets</u> too — <u>food producers</u> often make it a <u>big deal</u> on their packaging if they use ingredients from the <u>UK</u>.

When planning your meals look to source local, seasonal ingredients that are in season and haven't been shipped from around the world.

So it's <u>good</u> for the <u>environment</u>, but buying locally does have <u>downsides</u> too:

1) <u>Seasonal</u> food is <u>not available</u> all year round, e.g. strawberries are only available in the summer, so you have a <u>smaller selection</u> of products.

2) <u>Unpackaged</u> or <u>unpreserved</u> foods <u>spoil</u> faster — you have to use them <u>quickly</u>.

Carbon Footprint Measures Environmental Impact

1) Your <u>carbon footprint</u> measures the <u>impact</u> your lifestyle has on the <u>environment</u>.

2) It's given as the amount of <u>greenhouse gases</u> you <u>directly</u> and <u>indirectly</u> produce from burning fossil fuels for <u>heat</u>, <u>electricity</u>, <u>transport</u> etc. (usually expressed as <u>tonnes</u> of <u>carbon dioxide</u> per year).

3) <u>Foods</u> have a carbon footprint too — greenhouse gases are produced when <u>growing</u>, <u>processing</u>, <u>packaging</u> and <u>transporting</u> them.

The average UK person has a carbon footprint of over 10 tonnes a year.

You can <u>reduce</u> your carbon footprint:

- Buy food that is <u>in season</u>, with <u>lower food miles</u> and with <u>less packaging</u>
- Use <u>public transport</u>, <u>walk</u> or take up <u>cycling</u>
- <u>Waste less energy</u> in the home (e.g. turn TVs off standby, turn the heating down)

From plate to mouth — 0.0001 food miles...

Brussels sprouts come into season between October and March, so they're perfect for Christmas dinners (and are the best bit of course) — buying seasonally means tastier food and cuts down on food miles from importing them.

Q1 Explain the benefits of 'pick your own' strawberries over buying from a supermarket. [3 marks]

Q2 a) Give an example of a food product that has a high carbon footprint. [1 mark]

b) Explain why your chosen food product has a high carbon footprint. [2 marks]

Global Food Production

A great <u>challenge</u> we face today is to provide the world's <u>population</u> with a <u>steady</u>, <u>sustainable</u> supply of food. You need to understand <u>why</u> this is such a challenge and know the effect <u>climate change</u> is having.

Food Production Contributes to Climate Change...

1) <u>Processing</u>, <u>transporting</u> and <u>wasting</u> food all lead to the production of <u>greenhouse gases</u>.

2) These greenhouse gases <u>build up</u> in the <u>atmosphere</u>.

3) Heat is '<u>trapped</u>' — less heat can <u>escape</u> into space.

4) This effect is what is causing <u>global warming</u> — the Earth is getting slowly hotter.

5) <u>Rising temperatures</u> are changing our <u>climate</u>, causing more <u>extreme</u> weather (e.g. <u>hurricanes</u>, <u>tornadoes</u>) than usual.

6) Changes in the <u>temperature</u> and <u>weather</u> are affecting the <u>crops</u> and <u>food</u> that we <u>rely</u> on.

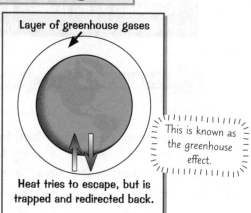

Layer of greenhouse gases

Heat tries to escape, but is trapped and redirected back.

This is known as the greenhouse effect.

...and Climate Change Can Affect Food Production

1) Just a <u>tiny increase</u> in average global <u>temperature</u> can <u>massively affect</u> the production of <u>crops</u>:

- Many crops will have <u>lower yields</u>, e.g. maize production could be reduced by millions of tonnes.
- <u>Pests</u> and <u>microorganisms</u> can reproduce more easily and can <u>invade</u> new regions that were <u>too cold</u> for them before.

2) <u>Climate change</u> can cause some <u>extreme weather events</u> which affect food production:

Drought

- A drought happens in an area that has had a <u>lack of rainfall</u>.
- Crops <u>struggle</u> to grow or <u>fail completely</u>.
- Rivers and lakes can dry up, <u>killing fish</u> and other <u>wildlife</u>.
- Drought can cause <u>wildfires</u> — uncontrollable fires <u>spread</u> through the countryside, <u>destroying fields</u> and <u>reared animals</u>.

Flooding

- <u>Severe rainfall</u>, <u>cyclones</u> etc. can cause major flooding.
- Floods directly <u>damage</u> and <u>destroy</u> crops.
- <u>Soil</u> and <u>nutrients</u> useful for crop growth are <u>washed away</u>.
- <u>Sewage</u> can <u>pollute</u> fields and spread <u>disease</u> in animals.
- Reared animals may <u>drown</u>.

3) In certain parts of the world, <u>food shortages</u> are <u>common</u> due to <u>droughts</u> (e.g. Ethiopia) or <u>flooding</u> (e.g. Bangladesh).

4) The lack of food leads to <u>malnutrition</u> (due to a diet without the right balance of nutrients), <u>ill health</u> and even <u>death</u> from <u>starvation</u>.

<u>Some colder countries</u> may <u>benefit</u> from a warmer climate — they can grow things that they <u>couldn't before</u>. E.g. <u>more land</u> is being used for <u>wine grapes</u> in southern <u>England</u> due to recent warm summers.

Today's forecast — flooding with a shortage of meatballs...

We snuck in a page from our Geography revision guide to see if you'd notice. Surprise! I kid... but while this is all climate change chat, remember this <u>is</u> a food book, so you need to link everything to food production.

Q1 Give one way that rising sea levels could affect food production.

[1 mark]

Global Food Production

Resources, such as food, water and energy, are necessary for a basic standard of living — with the world's population rapidly increasing there is a greater demand for these resources.

Food Security is Where People Have Access to Food They Need

People have food security when they have access to enough nutritious food to stay healthy and active.

You can talk about the food security of a person, a community or a whole country:

A country that can produce a lot of food or is rich enough to import the food it needs has food security.

An African village where the people can't produce enough food or buy what they need does not have food security.

Many factors affect how much food is available.

- Climate — some countries have climates that are unsuitable for farming (e.g. too hot, too cold, or too little rainfall). Extreme weather events, such as floods or droughts, can also affect the food supply.
- Insufficient land — people living in poverty don't have their own land to grow food.
- Growing industrial crops — more farmland that previously grew crops for food is now being used to grow non-food crops, e.g. crops for biofuels (fuels from plant material).
- Wealth — wealthier people have more disposable income to spend on food, often more than they need. People with lower incomes may not be able to afford nutritious food.
- Rising population — the more people there are, the less food there is to go around.

We Need to Produce More Food

With global demand for food increasing, we need to increase food supplies.

- Using new technologies — e.g. GM crops can be given pest-resistance, higher nutritional values and higher yields.
- Eating less meat — animals that are reared for their meat are fed crops that we grow. It's more efficient if we directly eat those crops instead.
- Reducing food waste — if less food is wasted, more is available to eat.

And we have to use sustainable techniques (e.g. when fishing — p.58) which don't damage the environment or use up limited resources, so that enough food can continue to be grown to feed future generations.

Fairtrade is About Improving Conditions for Farmers

1) The Fairtrade Foundation was established to support farmers and workers in less developed countries and encourage sustainable food production.

2) Raw ingredients (such as tea leaves, coffee beans etc.) are used in expensive products — but the farmers often receive very little money for their produce.

3) Fairtrade aims to make it fairer for these smaller businesses by making sure they get a decent price and by improving working conditions.

4) The farmers themselves become more food secure — they have more money to spend on food for themselves and their families.

5) Look for the FAIRTRADE mark on products like coffee and tea.

Don't let food security cashew stealing any nuts...

Food security is a strange term but all it means is whether someone has access to plenty of nutritious food. Learn the factors that affect it too — you won't solve world hunger but it will help you write a great exam answer.

Q1 Sienna lives in the UK and earns a high income.
Explain whether you think Sienna does or does not have food security. [3 marks]

Primary Food Processing

Primary processing prepares raw foods (straight from being picked, harvested or slaughtered) so they're ready either to be eaten or cooked immediately or used as ingredients to make other food products.

Fruit, Vegetables and Meat Undergo Basic Processing

All food is processed in some way before it reaches our plate. It's important so that food is safe to eat, is easier to transport, doesn't spoil as quickly and looks nice for the consumer. For example:

Fruit
- Pits (stones) are removed from fruit, e.g. peaches and cherries.
- Fruits are squeezed for fruit juices or dried, e.g. grapes are sun-dried to make raisins.

Veg
- Vegetables are washed with water to remove dirt, insects and chemical sprays.
- Vegetables are sorted into different sizes and shapes and may be peeled.

Poultry
- Feathers and internal organs are removed.
- The wings and legs are tied (trussed) so it cooks evenly.

Meat
- Some meats (e.g. beef) are hung and dried to make it more tender and improve flavour.
- Meat is chopped, sliced or cut.

Flour is Made by Milling Wheat Grains

A wheat grain
Bran (mostly fibre)
Endosperm (mostly starch)
Germ (vitamins, protein and fat)

1) A wheat grain contains different parts — the bran, endosperm and germ.
2) Wheat grains (seeds) are harvested and then cleaned to remove any stones, dust etc.
3) The grains are stored in dry conditions to prevent moulds from growing on them.
4) The grains are put into a hopper and are crushed between rollers that crack open the grain.
5) Different types of flour can be made by sieving and removing parts of the grain.

> Wholemeal flour — 100% of the grain is used, nothing is taken out.
> Wheatmeal (Brown) flour — about 85% of the grain is used, some of the bran and germ are removed.
> White flour — about 70% of the grain is used (only the endosperm is used).

6) Important B group vitamins are lost when making white flour, so they're added back in (p.66).
7) The Eatwell Guide recommends wholemeal products as we get the nutritional benefit of the whole grain.

Milk is Heat Treated to Kill Bacteria

Milk is heat treated to destroy pathogenic bacteria, but other non-harmful bacteria are also lost.

Pasteurisation — milk is heated quickly to 72 °C for 15 seconds and then rapidly cooled. There is little change in the taste and nutritional content of pasteurised milk.

Ultra Heat Treatment (UHT) — milk is heated to at least 135 °C for 1-4 seconds and packed in a sterile container — the milk can last at an ambient (see p.37) temperature for several months. UHT milk has slightly less nutritional value and a slightly different taste than pasteurised milk.

Sterilisation — bottled raw milk goes through a steam chamber at 110 °C for 10-30 minutes. ALL bacteria are killed, so it tastes different, and many B group vitamins and vitamin C are lost.

Microfiltration (MF) — bacteria that turn milk sour remain after pasteurisation. Microfiltration forces milk through a membrane which separates the milk from the souring bacteria. This extends the shelf life of the milk and doesn't have much effect on the flavour or nutritional content.

Secondary Food Processing

Secondary Processing Uses Primary Processed Foods

After primary processing comes, surprisingly, secondary processing. Primary processed foods are turned into other food products by altering them in some way or combining them with other ingredients.

There are some important secondary processes you need to learn:

Raw food

↓

Primary processing

↓

Secondary processing

Flour is Turned into Pasta

1) Pasta is made with a mixture of water (or eggs) and semolina flour.

2) The ingredients form a dough which is kneaded until it is smooth.

3) Colourings can be added to dye the pasta — spinach makes it green, beetroot makes it purple and carrot makes an orange pasta.

4) The dough is then shaped — it is forced through a metal die and then folded or twisted to make different types of pasta.

5) Pasta can be sold fresh or dried. Dried pasta has a much longer shelf life — all the moisture in the pasta is taken out.

Semolina flour comes from milling a type of wheat known as durum wheat.

You also need to know how flour is processed to make bread — see p.32.

Fruit is Turned into Jam

1) Jam is a type of fruit preserve — it is made with crushed fruit, sugar and pectin.

2) Pectin is a gelling substance found in fruit — when boiled (to at least 105 °C) with the sugar and acid of the fruit, pectin causes the jam to thicken and set as it cools.

3) The sugar draws water out of the fruit, so it's difficult for microorganisms to grow.

4) Jam is poured into glass jars which are sealed to further extend the shelf life — jam is an ambient food that can be stored for several months without going off.

Processes such as boiling and drying remove important nutrients in foods. In jam making, for example, high temperatures will destroy vitamin C in the fruit.

Milk is Turned into Cheese

You also need to know how milk is processed to make yoghurt — see p.40.

1 For most types of cheese, raw milk is pasteurised to kill off any pathogenic bacteria.

Bacteria   Rennet

2 'Friendly' bacteria sour and thicken the milk and rennet from calf stomachs is added. A vegetarian alternative to rennet can be used.

Curds

Whey

3 Rennet causes the milk to coagulate into solid cheese curds. The liquid remaining is called whey.

4 The whey is removed by either draining, cutting, cooking, salting or stacking curds on top of each other (cheddaring).

5 The curds are pressed to form blocks of cheese and placed in temperature-controlled storage to 'mature' and develop taste and texture.

6 Bacteria or moulds may be added to change the flavour of the cheese (see p.40).

No whey — he's fallen at the final curdle...

Two cheese puns in one — I do like to treat you sometimes. Wrap your head around primary and secondary food processing and the important examples of each, then leap over these hurdles (disguised as lovely questions).

Q1   Give two examples of primary processing of fish.   [2 marks]

Q2   Explain why bread is an example of a food that has undergone secondary processing.   [3 marks]

Food Fortification and Modification

Manufacturers have the technology nowadays to modify food products to give additional health benefits.

Fortification Adds Nutrients to a Food

1) Fortification is where nutrients are added to a food.
2) It improves the nutritional value of foods.
3) Fortification is done for different reasons — sometimes it's to replace nutrients lost during processing or to add extra nutrients to make it healthier.
4) There are some examples you need to know:

Take a look through p.1–10 to see why we need nutrients in our diet.

White Flour

- Iron, thiamin (B1), niacin (B3) and calcium are lost during the production of white flour (p.64).
- By law, these nutrients have to be added back in — they aren't added to wholemeal flour because the nutrients are naturally present.

Breakfast Cereals

- Cereals can be fortified with iron, thiamin and folic acid.
- Cereal is eaten by lots of people — if manufacturers choose to fortify their products it helps the population get the recommended amounts of these nutrients.

WHEATY BITS

With added:
Iron
Thiamin
Folic Acid

"If you can't wheat'em, eat'em."

Butter Alternatives

- Many people use butter alternatives, e.g. margarine and low-fat spreads.
- Butter naturally contains vitamins A and D — by fortifying butter alternatives, consumers don't miss out on these important vitamins.
- Margarine and low-fat spreads are usually fortified on a voluntary basis by manufacturers.

Cholesterol Lowering Spreads

- Some vegetable fat spreads have added plant sterols.
- These substances help reduce cholesterol for people with high cholesterol only — they don't benefit people with normal cholesterol levels.

5) Manufacturers may fortify processed foods as a 'marketing tool' — it can give the impression that their products are healthy.
6) You should be careful eating excessive amounts of fortified foods — you may get too much of some vitamins or minerals in your diet.

DOUGHNUTS
1 of your
5 a day!

Multivitamin supplements are hugely popular:

- Multivitamin supplements are full of vitamins and minerals your body needs — they're handy if you don't get enough from your normal diet but should never replace a healthy, balanced diet.
- They are more useful for certain people, e.g. elderly adults (see p.13) and pregnant women.
- However, it's debatable whether they make any difference for most people and taking too many could be harmful to your health.

Cramming doughnuts with vitamins? Modify can help it...

"But CGP, why can't we just add vitamins to junk food to make it healthy?" Unfortunately, this isn't going to make junk food magically any healthier — remember, these foods are still packed with sugar, salt and fats. Sad face.

Q1   Explain why a milk substitute like soya milk might be fortified.   [2 marks]

Q2   Gerardo's diet consists of many fortified foods.
         Explain why Gerardo should be careful taking vitamin supplements with his normal diet.   [2 marks]

Food Fortification and Modification

There are other ways of improving food products so they're nicer than ever — mmm, read on...

Additives Change the Properties of Food

1) An additive is something that's added to food to improve its properties.
2) Some additives occur naturally and some are made artificially.

Preservatives are additives that prevent bacteria from growing — so the food lasts longer.
- Natural preservatives include vinegar, lemon juice, salt and sugar.
- Artificial preservatives include things like nitrates and sulphites.

> Important in food safety — see p.34

Colourings make food look more attractive and more appealing to eat. They can be used to add colour to something that is colourless, or to return food to its natural colour if it's lost during processing.
- Caramel is a natural food colouring — it can make products darkish brown, e.g. cola.
- Tartrazine is an artificial food colouring — it's used to make products a yellow colour, e.g. custard powder, syrups, sweets.

> Tartrazine combined with a blue colouring produces the green used for mushy peas.

Flavourings improve the taste or the aroma (smell) of a product.
- Natural flavourings include herbs and spices, e.g. basil, chillies and vanilla.
- Artificial sweeteners, e.g. aspartame, are used as substitutes for sugar.
- Monosodium glutamate (MSG) enhances flavours of foods it is used in — it boosts the existing flavour of a product and gives it a savoury taste.

> Natural sugar alternatives like xylitol and stevia are becoming more popular now, e.g. in soft drinks.

Emulsifiers and stabilisers help preserve the shape and texture of food products (see p.31). Emulsifiers help mix together ingredients that don't usually mix, e.g. oily and watery liquids. Stabilisers stop mixed ingredients from separating.
- Lecithin is a natural emulsifier found in egg yolks and soya beans.
- Pectin is a natural stabiliser found in berries, apples and many other fruits.

Additives Have Disadvantages Too

1) Additives, such as sulphites (found in bacon or salami), can cause allergic reactions and worsen asthma.
2) Some natural additives, like sugar and salt, are bad for our health in large amounts.
3) They can disguise poor quality ingredients, e.g. processed meat products may not contain much meat but can be made to taste good by using additives.
4) Additives must pass a safety test before they can be used in food — when an additive passes it gets an E number and can be used throughout the European Union, e.g. caramel colouring is E150a...
5) ...but there are concerns about possible long-term health effects. Some research suggests that at least six colourings: sunset yellow (E110), quinoline yellow (E104), carmoisine (E122), allura red (E129), tartrazine (E102), and ponceau 4R (E124) cause hyperactive behaviour in children.

This sentence needs an emulsifier...

Food additives are really handy and lots of processed foods are chockablock with them, but there is concern about the long term health effects that some additives may cause.

Q1   Explain why a manufacturer might add colourings to sweets.   [1 mark]

Q2   Give three reasons why a consumer might choose a frozen lasagne with no artificial additives.   [3 marks]

Revision Questions for Section Five

I can't believe it's another one of these revision question pages already — you know the drill by now.
Put on your food provenance cap and start working through these <u>section 5</u> questions.

- Try these questions and <u>tick off each one</u> when you <u>get it right</u>.
- When you've done <u>all the questions</u> for a topic and are <u>completely happy</u> with it, tick off the topic.

<u>Grown, Reared and Caught Food (p.55-58)</u> ☑

1) What is meant by 'intensive farming'? ☑
2) Give one disadvantage of using pesticides. ☑
3) Describe an alternative to using a pesticide as a method of controlling pests. ☑
4) What is meant by 'organic farming'? ☑
5) What is a 'genetically modified' food? ☑
6) List five advantages and three disadvantages of growing GM foods. ☑
7) Explain the difference between a 'factory-farmed' and a 'free-range' animal. ☑
8) What does the 'Red Tractor' symbol mean on food packaging? ☑
9) Describe two different fishing methods. ☑
10) Explain how unsustainable fishing can damage the environment. ☑

<u>Waste Food and Packaging (p.59-60)</u> ☑

11) List lots of ways that food is wasted a) in the home b) by producers and retailers. ☑
12) Explain why using excessive packaging is bad for the environment. ☑
13) List three ways that we can help to reduce food packaging waste. ☑

<u>Food Miles, Carbon Footprint and Global Food Production (p.61-63)</u> ☑

14) What is meant by 'food miles'? ☑
15) Give a reason why bananas are imported to the UK. ☑
16) List four advantages and two disadvantages of only buying local food. ☑
17) Name three things that increase your carbon footprint. ☑
18) Briefly describe how food production contributes to climate change. ☑
19) For each weather event, explain how it affects food production: a) drought   b) flooding ☑
20) What is meant by 'food security'? ☑
21) Explain a factor that affects the food security of a: a) person   b) country ☑
22) Describe what the Fairtrade Foundation is. ☑

<u>Food Processing, Fortification and Modification (p.64-67)</u> ☑

23) Give two examples of primary processing of vegetables. ☑
24) Explain the differences between wholemeal flour, wheatmeal flour and white flour. ☑
25) Describe the following procedures used in the primary processing of milk:
    a) pasteurisation   b) UHT   c) sterilisation   d) microfiltration ☑
26) Explain how these food products are made: a) pasta   b) jam   c) cheese ☑
27) What is meant by food 'fortification'? List four food products that are commonly fortified. ☑
28) Give an example for each type of additive and say what it does.
    a) preservatives   b) colourings   c) flavourings   d) emulsifiers   e) stabilisers ☑
29) List four disadvantages of using food additives. ☑

Practical Skills

A note about this section

On these pages we'll cover all the <u>practical skills</u> you need to learn for AQA.
You should have practised all these skills during your course — this is just a <u>brief reminder</u>.
If there are any that you're <u>rusty</u> on, it's time to do some <u>brushing up</u>.

- Make sure you have a <u>good knowledge</u> of all of these skills for your <u>exam</u>.
- You'll also need to <u>demonstrate a good range</u> of these skills in your <u>non-exam assessment</u>.

Skill 1: General Practical Skills

Weigh and Measure Ingredients Accurately

1) <u>Dry ingredients</u> (e.g. flour) and <u>solid ingredients</u> (e.g. butter) are usually measured using <u>electronic</u> or <u>balance weighing scales</u>.

2) <u>Liquids</u> are measured in <u>measuring jugs</u> or <u>cups</u> (some dry ingredients are measured in cups too).

3) You can use <u>measuring spoons</u> (e.g. a teaspoon) for small amounts.

Prepare Your Workspace

1) It's a good idea to <u>organise</u> all your ingredients and equipment <u>before</u> you start <u>cooking</u> (e.g. weighing and measuring out your ingredients).

2) You can also <u>grease</u>, <u>oil</u>, <u>line</u> or <u>flour</u> equipment like tins — this not only makes removing the food easier, but it also helps with cleaning up after.

Select and Adapt Cooking Times

1) <u>Cooking time</u> is affected by different factors, including the <u>type of food</u> (e.g. fish cooks a lot faster than red meat) and <u>portion size</u> (e.g. a thick piece of steak needs cooking for longer than a thin one).

2) Select an <u>appropriate</u> cooking time, but be prepared to <u>adapt</u> it — e.g. if your food is cooking quicker than expected, reduce the cooking time (but make sure that you cook it thoroughly all the way through to the middle).

Test Food to See If It's Cooked

You need to be able to tell if food is <u>cooked through</u> properly. Luckily, there are ways to check this:

- <u>Temperature probes</u> are placed into the middle of food to check if it's <u>hot enough</u> (see p.38).

- You can pop <u>knives</u> or <u>skewers</u> into food such as cake mixtures — if they come out <u>clean</u> then the mixture is cooked.

- You can also cut into <u>meats</u> and apply a little pressure — if the <u>juices</u> come out <u>clear</u> (without blood) the food is cooked.

- You can <u>gently press</u> cakes to see if they're cooked. The cake is done if it <u>springs back</u> when you poke it.

- When cooking foods like pasta, you can <u>bite</u> into a small piece to see if it's cooked to your liking. But be warned — too much use of the bite test can quickly result in small meals.

- If you've ever baked biscuits until they were '<u>golden brown</u>', you've successfully completed a <u>visual colour check</u>.

Testing Testing, 1, 2, 3

- You can also perform a <u>sound check</u> by knocking on the bottom of baked bread — if it's baked correctly you should hear a hollow sound.

Practical Skills

Change How Food Affects the Senses

In Task 2 of the non-exam assessment (see p.78) it's important to get the seasoning right or you'll lose marks.

1) You can change and improve the flavour of foods with <u>salt</u>, <u>pepper</u>, <u>sugar</u>, <u>herbs</u> and <u>spices</u>, but also by using:

   - <u>Pastes</u> (e.g. garlic paste)
   - <u>Reductions</u> (see p.73)
   - <u>Jus</u> (a thin sauce made from the juices of cooked meat)
   - <u>Infused oils</u> (oils that have absorbed the flavour of herbs)

When cooking, try a small amount of your food to see how it tastes. You can then adjust it until the flavour is right.

2) The <u>texture</u> of food can be changed by adding <u>crust</u>, <u>crispiness</u> and <u>crumbs</u>, e.g. coating chicken in breadcrumbs, adding seeds to bread dough or breadcrumbs on top of a dish, e.g. macaroni cheese.

3) <u>Browning</u> changes the <u>flavour</u> and <u>appearance</u> of food:

   - Both <u>dextrinisation</u> and <u>caramelisation</u> brown food (see p.29).
   - You can even use a cook's <u>blowtorch</u> to brown the tops of foods, e.g. a crème brûlée.
   - You can <u>glaze</u> foods (e.g. pies) by <u>brushing egg</u> over the food. When it cooks, the pie will have a nice golden brown colour.

Jeff always wanted to be a painter...

Add Garnishes and Decorate Your Dishes

1) <u>Garnishes</u> are small <u>additions</u> to your dish and can <u>add extra colour</u> and/or <u>flavour</u>. These can be as <u>simple or complicated</u> as you want, from a slice of lemon or a piece of lettuce to a piped balsamic sauce or a flower made out of a radish.

2) Other <u>decorative techniques</u> can be used, such as <u>piping</u> icing onto a cake, or creating a decorative <u>pattern</u> on top of a pie.

3) Styling your food using these techniques can make your dish look <u>more appealing</u>.

Skill 2: Knife Skills

Different Knives Are Used for Different Jobs

You need a variety of <u>knives</u> for all the <u>different skills</u> you use when preparing food:

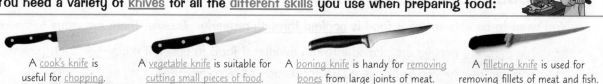

A <u>cook's knife</u> is useful for <u>chopping</u>.

A <u>vegetable knife</u> is suitable for <u>cutting small pieces of food</u>.

A <u>boning knife</u> is handy for <u>removing bones</u> from large joints of meat.

A <u>filleting knife</u> is used for removing fillets of meat and fish.

It's <u>REALLY IMPORTANT</u> to <u>take care</u> when using these knives as they can cause serious harm.

There Are Different Ways to Cut Fruit and Vegetables

1) When cutting <u>smaller fruits and vegetables</u> (e.g. apples or potatoes) use a <u>bridge hold</u>.

2) When cutting <u>longer fruits and vegetables</u> (e.g. carrots or cucumbers) use a <u>claw grip</u>. It's really important that your <u>fingers</u> are <u>tucked under</u> here so they don't get sliced off.

3) You can use a knife to <u>peel</u>, <u>slice</u> and <u>dice</u> (chop into small cubes) your fruit and veg. Or cut them into <u>batons</u> (thick sticks) or, to be fancier, <u>julienne</u> strips (thin sticks).

Practical Skills

Cutting Meat and Fish Is More Complicated

1) Cutting meat and fish is more complicated and requires a different approach to cutting fruit and veg. It also requires a different type of knife, e.g. a <u>boning</u> or <u>filleting knife</u> (see previous page).

2) You can <u>divide</u> a <u>whole chicken</u> into eight portions (two of each of the following: drumsticks, thighs, breasts and wings). The chicken breasts are then often <u>filleted</u> (this removes the skin and tenderloin).

There are loads of video tutorials online that show you how to portion and fillet various foods with step-by-step instructions.

3) Different methods of filleting are needed for <u>round</u> fish (e.g. mackerel) and <u>flatfish</u> (e.g. plaice) due to the position of the backbone. You'll typically get 2 fillets (pieces) from round fish, and 4 from flatfish.

4) Knives can be used to remove <u>fat</u> and <u>rind</u> (the thick skin of foods such as pork).

Skill 3: Preparing Fruit and Vegetables

1) You probably already know (and use) lots of the different ways you can prepare fruit and veg.

2) Some of the <u>most common</u> include: <u>mashing</u>, <u>crushing</u>, <u>shredding</u>, <u>grating</u>, <u>peeling</u>, <u>de-seeding</u> and <u>blending</u>.

3) Other methods include:

Blanching, scooping, de-skinning — sounds like something from a horror movie to me...

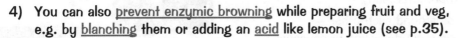

- <u>Segmenting</u> — e.g. <u>dividing an orange</u> into segments.
- <u>Piping</u> — e.g. <u>piping mash</u> to create decorative patterns.
- <u>Blanching</u> — placing the fruit or veg into <u>boiling</u> then <u>cold water</u> (see p.24).
- <u>De-skinning</u> — this can be done by blanching tomatoes (after blanching, the skins can be <u>peeled off</u> easily just using your fingertips).
- <u>Scooping</u> — this is used when <u>balling melons</u> or making <u>equal portions</u> of <u>mash</u>.
- <u>Juicing</u> — e.g. using a <u>lemon squeezer</u>.
- <u>Preparing garnishes</u> — e.g. <u>tomato roses</u> that go alongside a main dish.
- <u>Scissor snipping</u> — e.g. when <u>snipping herbs</u>. You can use special <u>herb scissors</u> that have <u>multiple blades</u> to make snipping even quicker.

4) You can also <u>prevent enzymic browning</u> while preparing fruit and veg, e.g. by <u>blanching</u> them or adding an <u>acid</u> like lemon juice (see p.35).

Skill 4: Use of the Cooker (and Skill 6: Cooking Methods)

The technical side of the <u>cooking methods</u> below have been covered in <u>Section 2</u>, but here's a quick recap on how you can use your cooker's <u>grill</u>, <u>oven</u> and <u>hob</u>:

Well hello me!

Grill
- The cooker can grill food such as <u>meat</u>, <u>fish</u>, <u>veg</u> and <u>firm cheese</u> like <u>halloumi</u> (see p.26).
- You can also use the grill to <u>char</u> (blacken the outside) and <u>toast</u> foods, e.g. seeds and nuts.

Oven
- The <u>oven</u> can be used for <u>baking</u> (p.26), <u>roasting</u> (p.27) and <u>braising</u> (p.25).
- You can also use it to cook <u>casseroles</u> and <u>tagines</u>. Both are <u>slow-cooked</u> to <u>tenderise</u> the meat inside. Like braising, they cook food in a mix of liquid, vegetables and herbs. A <u>tagine</u> is a <u>slow-cooked North African dish</u> that's cooked in a covered pot which (confusingly) is also called a tagine. Both casseroles and tagines are <u>covered</u> during cooking to trap moisture.

A tagine... in... a tagine

Hob
- <u>Water-based</u> hob methods include <u>steaming</u>, <u>boiling</u>, <u>simmering</u>, <u>blanching</u> and <u>poaching</u> (p.24).
- <u>Fat-based</u> hob methods include <u>stir-frying</u> and <u>shallow frying</u> (p.25).
- The hob is also used for <u>dry frying</u>, sometimes called <u>dry roasting</u> (p.27).

Practical Skills

Skill 5: Use of Equipment

Equipment Can Be Used to Save Time

1) <u>Blenders</u> are used to <u>blend</u> (chop and mix) different ingredients together. This makes them good for <u>soups</u> and <u>smoothies</u>. They come in many different forms: some are a jug with a rotating blade, while with others you lower the blade into the food <u>by hand</u>.

2) <u>Food processors</u> are similar to blenders but they can be used for <u>mixing</u>, <u>slicing</u>, <u>chopping</u>, <u>grinding</u> and <u>dicing</u> food. Using the <u>same settings</u> will give you the <u>same results</u> each time. They're good for making burgers, meatballs, quickly chopping onions or (with an attachment) grating carrots.

3) <u>Food mixers</u> (unsurprisingly) mix food. They're often used for making <u>cake mixtures</u> and <u>batters</u>. Like blenders, they can be <u>hand-held</u> or come as a worktop appliance with a mixing bowl attached.

4) <u>Pasta machines</u> have <u>rollers</u> that turn your <u>pasta dough</u> into flat <u>sheets of pasta</u>. They can usually be adjusted to change the <u>thickness</u> of the pasta and create <u>different types</u> of pasta.

5) <u>Microwave ovens</u> use <u>radiation</u> (see p.23) to <u>quickly</u> cook foods such as baked potato and to heat up foods such as baked beans. They're also good for quickly <u>melting</u> foods like chocolate and cheese.

Not to be used as a laundry mangle...

Skill 7: Prepare, Combine and Shape

Mixtures for burgers, fish cakes and meatballs often include eggs — when the food is cooked, the proteins in the eggs coagulate (see p.28) and bind the mixture together.

1) You can <u>shape</u> and bind <u>wet</u> mixtures <u>by hand</u>, e.g. shaping burgers, fish cakes, meatballs, or doughs for biscuits or bread buns — it's quick, but your results might not be very consistent.

2) You can also <u>combine</u> different foods in a variety of ways to make your dishes more interesting:

- You can <u>wrap</u> foods around each other — e.g. wrapping bacon around chicken or sausages.

Chickens in blankets anyone?

- Foods including meat, vegetables and fruit can be <u>skewered</u> together to make <u>kebabs</u>.

Vegetable kebab

- Different types of <u>rolls</u> can be made — e.g. sushi, sausage rolls and spring rolls.

Maki roll

- You can <u>coat</u> foods with different ingredients — e.g. coating chicken pieces, fish or cheese by covering them in flour, then egg, then breadcrumbs.

Chicken in breadcrumbs

- Foods can also be combined by <u>layering</u> them. A popular example is <u>lasagne</u>, although layering can also be achieved more simply — e.g. the mashed potato on the top of a <u>shepherd's pie</u>.

Lasagne

Shape it! Mix it! Roll it! Bind it!

Experimenting with how you can shape, combine and cook food is a heck of a lot of fun. Without the invention of unusual ideas, we wouldn't have the delicious combinations we have today — chocolate on pizza, for example.

Practical Skills

Now if this stuff doesn't get you excited, I don't know what will. Seriously though, this stuff is <u>dead useful</u>.

Skill 8: Sauce Making

Sauces can be Made in Lots of Different Ways

Sauces are used in both savoury and sweet dishes — as an <u>accompaniment</u> (e.g. custard, ketchup) or as <u>part</u> of the dish (e.g. in lasagne). You can put pretty much anything you like in a sauce, but they usually contain at least one of these: <u>flour</u>, <u>butter</u>, <u>eggs</u>, <u>cornflour</u>, <u>stock</u>, <u>milk</u>, <u>cream</u>, <u>sugar</u>. Here are three ways you can make a sauce:

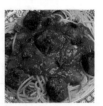

Gelatinisation Thickens Starch-Based Sauces

Starch-based sauces thicken by <u>gelatinisation</u> (see p.29). They can be made in different ways:

You can make a <u>roux</u> as a base for your sauce by mixing equal weights of <u>melted butter</u> and <u>plain flour</u> in a pan — stir until the flour is <u>cooked</u> (to add colour and get rid of the raw flour taste). Gradually add <u>liquid</u> (e.g. milk) to make a sauce, stirring to avoid lumps the whole time. <u>Simmer</u>, then add the rest of your ingredients. The roux will help to give your sauce a good <u>consistency</u> (thickness) and <u>flavour</u>.

To make a <u>blended sauce</u>, you mix <u>cornflour</u> with a small amount of <u>water/milk</u> to form a paste (a blend of starch and liquid). You then heat up additional liquid and add it to the paste to make a sauce. <u>Heat</u> the sauce until it <u>thickens</u>.

Or you can just make an <u>all-in-one</u> sauce by putting all your ingredients into a saucepan. <u>Stir</u> over a medium heat, until your sauce starts to bubble and thicken.

You can adapt a plain roux sauce to make an <u>infused velouté</u> sauce or a <u>béchamel</u> sauce:

- A <u>velouté sauce</u> is made by adding <u>white stock</u> (e.g. chicken or fish stock) to the roux <u>instead of milk</u>.
- For a <u>béchamel sauce</u>, you simmer the milk with foods such as <u>peppercorns</u>, <u>onions</u>, <u>cloves</u> and <u>bay leaves</u>.

The <u>thickness</u> of your sauce depends on the <u>ratio of starch to liquid</u> in it, e.g. the more milk you add to your roux, the thinner your sauce will become. This has many different uses, such as using a <u>thick</u> roux sauce to <u>bind ingredients together</u> in a fish cake, or making a <u>thin pouring sauce</u>, e.g. cheese sauce.

Reduction Sauces Thicken by Evaporation

You can include liquids like cooking juices, stock and wine in reduction sauces.

1) Reduction is a process that <u>thickens liquids</u> such as <u>sauces</u> and soups by <u>simmering</u> them and causing water to <u>evaporate</u> — this also <u>concentrates</u> the <u>flavour</u> of the sauce, making it more <u>intense</u>.

2) Common reduction sauces include <u>tomato pasta sauce</u>, <u>curry sauce</u> and <u>gravy</u>, although they can also be sweet-tasting — such as apple or raspberry <u>coulis</u>.

Emulsion Sauces Contain Oil and Water

There's loads of stuff about <u>emulsion sauces</u> (e.g. hollandaise) on <u>p.31</u>.

Skill 9: Tenderise and Marinate

1) <u>Marination</u> involves <u>soaking</u> vegetables, meat, fish or alternatives such as tofu in a <u>liquid</u> before they're cooked. This liquid often contains <u>herbs</u>, <u>spices</u> and <u>acid</u> (e.g. lemon juice).

2) The <u>acid</u> in <u>marinades</u> makes meat <u>more tender</u> by <u>denaturing protein</u> (see p.28).

3) Marinades also add <u>flavour</u> and <u>moisture</u> to food. It's common for foods such as chicken to be paired with <u>barbecue</u>, <u>sweet chilli</u> or <u>tandoori marinades</u>.

Marinated tofu changes colour as it absorbs the marinade.

Practical Skills

Skill 10: Dough

Dough Making Uses Lots of Technical Skills

1) You need to make doughs whenever you make foods like bread, pastry and pasta.
2) Most doughs are made by combining flour, water and a bit of salt.
3) If you're making pasta dough, you can change the water for eggs.
4) Bread doughs also include yeast to give the final product a nice rise (p.32).
5) Fat or oil is added to change the texture of the dough — loads of it is used in pastry, and just a little in bread or pasta.
6) Making doughs can show you've learned lots of technical skills, including:

- Shortening (see p.30), e.g. if you were making shortcrust pastry.
- Forming gluten (see p.28), e.g. if you were kneading bread dough.
- Proving (see p.32), e.g. if you were making risen bread.

Different Types of Pastry Have Different Properties

When making pastry dough, you need to choose which one gives you the right taste and texture:

Type of pastry	Properties of finished pastry	Used for...
Shortcrust	A 'short' texture (see p.30)	pies, quiches, tarts and pasties
Sweet	Sweeter than other pastries	sweet pies and tarts
Puff	Has flaky, puffed up layers	sausage rolls, pies, fruit turnovers
Choux	Light texture and hollow centre	profiteroles and eclairs
Filo	Light, crisp and fragile	strudels and pastry parcels

Choux!

Each dough is different, and you need to think about different things for each one. E.g. when making choux pastry (for which the dough is more like a paste than other doughs), you need to cool the hot flour/butter mixture before adding your eggs (to avoid protein coagulation), and make sure you use enough water and a hot oven so that steam can be created and make the dough rise.

Shaping and Finishing Your Dough

When it comes to adding shape and finishing touches to your dough, there are a lot of options. Here's a big list of ways you could shape and finish your dough. You should know what each one is and be ready to demonstrate some in your non-exam assessment task.

- You can roll out doughs to get the right shape and thickness. Use a rolling pin to get an even thickness, and flour to stop the mixture sticking to surfaces.
- Folding a dough creates layers. This helps to trap air (p.32) and is used to make foods like puff pastries and palmiers.
- You can line cases with pastry dough (press the dough into the shape of the case — the dough then bakes into this shape, giving your pie a solid pastry case. You can prick the pastry with a fork to release any air and keep a flat base.

Palmiers

Lining a pastry tin

- Bread rolls can be shaped in a huge variety of ways, including: baguettes, bloomers, rings, bagels, cobs, braids, breadsticks, rolls etc...
- You can make different types of flatbread — lots of them don't use yeast (e.g. tortillas), although it's sometimes added to give them a relatively small rise (e.g. naan bread).

Practical Skills

- Choux pastry is used to make foods like profiteroles and chocolate eclairs — you can pipe it in different ways and shapes to create different products.

- Pasta dough can be shaped in lots of different ways to give us pasta like: ravioli, lasagne, cannelloni, tagliatelle, tortellini etc...

- Dough can be made into pinwheels by rolling it (not with a rolling pin, but in the same way you'd roll up a carpet). Cinnamon buns and cheesy pinwheels are made this way — you can even make coloured swirls by adding fillings.

- The most common shape for a pizza base is circular with thicker crusts around the outside. You can also make a calzone by folding the pizza over, completely covering the filling with dough.

- The shape of doughs change during proving as they rise and increase in size.
- Brushing your doughs with egg wash (egg mixed with water, milk or cream) creates a nice glaze that turns the food golden brown during baking.
- You can also finish the tops of pies and tarts using decorative patterns (p.70)

Skill 11: Raising Agents

Remember raising agents from p.32? Well, they're back for a lap of honour because they're just so darn useful. Just as a reminder, raising agents come in many different forms:

- Chemical (bicarbonate of soda, baking powder and self-raising flour), biological (yeast), mechanical (folding, beating, whisking, sieving, creaming and rubbing in) and steam.

- Eggs can also be used as a raising agent because their proteins stretch and trap air when they are whisked — this creates a gas-in-liquid foam that solidifies when the food is cooked (p.28).

Skill 12: Setting Mixtures

Gelation Sets Mixtures by Removing Heat

1) Foods such as custard or ice cream set when they are chilled or frozen.

2) This process is called gelation — this also happens with unbaked cheesecakes, as they need to be left in the fridge overnight to set.

3) It's easy to get confused between gelation and gelatinisation (p.29) — remember, gelation involves chilling, while gelatinisation involves heating.

Protein Coagulation Sets Egg-Based Mixtures

1) Mixtures that contain egg (e.g. quiches or egg custards) can be set by heating.

2) This is because when they're cooked, heat causes the proteins in the eggs to denature and coagulate (see p.28).

3) It's this coagulation of proteins in the mixture that causes it to set — it also traps the other ingredients in the mixture, e.g. bacon in quiche.

I heard this joke about margherita pizza — it was so cheesy...

There are a lot of different ways you can make, shape and finish your dough here — all these might seem a little overwhelming at first, but if you go through them one at a time (and maybe make a few of them) it will get easier.

Skills Checklist

So long <u>section 6</u> — there are a lot of practical skills on these pages, but it's important you can use them.

- Go through this list of practical skills and <u>tick off each one</u> when you <u>can do it</u>.
- When you can do <u>all the parts</u> of a skill section and are <u>completely happy</u> with it, tick it off.

<u>Skill 1: General Practical Skills (p.69-70)</u> ☑

1) I can weigh and measure ingredients accurately. ☑
2) I can organise all my ingredients before cooking. ☑
3) I can select and adapt cooking times. ☑
4) I can test food in a variety of ways to see if it's cooked. ☑
5) I can change how food affects the different senses. ☑
6) I can add garnishes and decoration to my food. ☑

<u>Skill 2: Knife Skills (p.70-71)</u> ☑

7) I can safely use different knives for different uses. ☑
8) I can cut fruit and vegetables in different ways. ☑
9) I know how chicken and fish can be portioned. ☑

<u>Skill 3: Preparing Fruit and Vegetables (p.71)</u> ☑

10) I can prepare fruit and vegetables in many different ways. ☑

<u>Skill 4: Use of the Cooker (and Skill 6: Cooking Methods) (p.71)</u> ☑

11) I can use the oven, grill and hob on the cooker for a range of cooking methods. ☑

<u>Skill 5: Use of Equipment (p.72)</u> ☑

12) I can use different equipment to speed up food preparation processes and save time. ☑

<u>Skill 7: Prepare, Combine and Shape (p.72)</u> ☑

13) I can prepare, shape and combine foods in a variety of ways. ☑

<u>Skill 8: Sauce Making (p.73)</u> ☑

14) I can make a roux, blended and all-in-one sauce. ☑
15) I can adapt a roux sauce to make a velouté and béchamel sauce. ☑
16) I can make a stable emulsion sauce. ☑
17) I can make both sweet and savoury reduction sauces. ☑

<u>Skill 9: Tenderise and Marinate (p.73)</u> ☑

18) I can make marinades to tenderise and flavour food. ☑

<u>Skill 10: Dough (p.74-75)</u> ☑

19) I can make a variety of different doughs using shortening, gluten formation and fermentation. ☑
20) I can select the right type of pastry dough for my dish. ☑
21) I can shape and finish my dough in lots of different ways. ☑

<u>Skill 11: Raising Agents (p.75)</u> ☑

22) I can use different raising agents to make my food rise. ☑

<u>Skill 12: Setting Mixtures (p.75)</u> ☑

23) I can set mixtures using gelation. ☑
24) I can set mixtures using eggs. ☑

Non-Exam Assessment Advice

In Food Preparation & Nutrition you'll have to do some cooking... and it'll be worth a good portion of the marks.

The Non-Exam Tasks Are Worth 50% of the Total Marks

1) During the final year of your GCSE, you'll have to do some <u>non-exam</u> tasks. They allow you to show off your <u>culinary knowledge</u> and <u>cooking skills</u>.

2) The non-exam work is split into <u>two</u> parts — a <u>Food Investigation task</u> worth 30 marks (15% of the course), and a <u>Food Preparation task</u> worth 70 marks (35% of the course).

The Food Investigation Task Involves Some Experimenting

1) In the Food Investigation task, you'll have to investigate and write a <u>report</u> about <u>how</u> and <u>why</u> ingredients work in a chosen task, e.g. "Investigate the ingredients used in sweet scone baking."

2) You'll be marked on three main things — <u>research</u>, <u>investigation</u> and <u>analysis</u>.

A — Research

1) Start by reading your task <u>thoroughly</u>, then draw out a <u>mind map</u> of the things you want to research — particularly how ingredients work, and why.

2) Use a <u>range of sources</u> to research your ideas, including textbooks, the internet and your own knowledge.

3) Use this research to make a <u>prediction</u> you can investigate — e.g. "Self-raising flour will be the best raising agent to use for making sweet scones."

Types of flour · Types of sugar · Types of filling, e.g. raisins, cherries · Amount of sugar · **Ingredients in scone baking** · Types of raising agent · Gluten content of different flours · Effects of using fresh / old milk · Essential scone ingredients

B — Investigation

1) To test your prediction you'll need to plan some <u>practical investigations</u>. You need to carry out <u>several experiments</u> (e.g. making scones with different flours, mechanically aerating scones in different ways).

2) It's important that these experiments have <u>clear methods</u> and are <u>fair</u>.

3) Prepare any <u>tables</u> or <u>graphs</u> to record your results in beforehand — this will make it clear what you need to write down during the experiments.

4) You should also take <u>photos</u> throughout your experiments to prove what you did.

> • E.g. Cook all at the same temperature, for the same length of time.
> • Make sure all ingredients are weighed accurately.
> • Make all scones the same size by using a cutter or weighing scale.

C — Analysis/Evaluation

1) You'll then need to <u>analyse</u> and <u>evaluate</u> your <u>findings</u> (interpret what you've discovered).

2) You can do this by <u>linking</u> your findings to the <u>research</u> you did at the start of the task (explaining how and why your ingredients worked the way they did), discussing your <u>results</u>, and deciding whether your findings support your <u>prediction</u> (is what happened what you expected?).

3) You need to show that you've done all this by producing a <u>written report</u>. This will include:

• A <u>summary</u> of your <u>research</u> (including how it helped you understand the task).

• Your <u>prediction</u> (including how your research led you to this decision).

• The <u>aims</u> of your different experiments (what you hoped to achieve).

• The <u>methods</u> you used in your experiments and how you made each one a <u>fair test</u>.

• The <u>ingredients</u> you used in your experiments.

• The <u>results</u> of your experiments (include any tables/graphs/charts here).

• Any <u>photos</u> you took during the task.

• An <u>analysis</u> of your results (this should fully explain what you have learned from them).

• A <u>conclusion</u> — this should sum up what you've learned, looking at your original predictions, results, how you'd apply what you've learned to future cooking projects, and any further research you'd do if you had the chance.

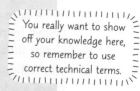
You really want to show off your knowledge here, so remember to use correct technical terms.

Non-Exam Assessment Advice

The Food Preparation Task Involves Lots of Cooking

1) In the <u>Food Preparation</u> task you'll have to cook a range of dishes to fit a chosen task, as well as producing a <u>portfolio</u> to show the following things:

- Your <u>research</u> (finding out more about your chosen task).
- The <u>practical skills</u> (e.g. different <u>technical skills/cooking techniques</u>) you're able to show by making <u>three</u> or <u>four dishes</u>, in an un-timed environment.
- Your ability to <u>prepare</u>, <u>cook</u> and <u>present three dishes</u> within a period of <u>3 hours</u>.
- An analysis of the <u>nutritional value</u>, <u>cost</u>, etc. of your chosen dishes.

2) During the practical tasks you should take <u>photographs</u> of each stage in the preparation and cooking. You will use these photographs in your <u>portfolio</u>.

Part 1 — Do the Research

1) First, make sure you've read all three tasks properly, then choose one that appeals to you. Each task on the brief has a certain <u>research focus</u>, such as '<u>life stages</u>', '<u>dietary requirements</u>' or '<u>cuisines</u>'. E.g. "Plan, prepare, cook and present a range of dishes which are suitable for vegans. Present three final dishes."

2) Decide what you need to research. This could be stuff like:

- <u>Advantages</u> and <u>disadvantages</u> of a vegan diet.
- <u>Meat</u> and <u>dairy-free</u> alternatives to everyday food products, and their nutritional values, e.g. soya milk, sunflower spread.
- <u>Surveying</u> vegans to ask about their personal food choices and / or the availability of vegan products.
- <u>Nutritional guidelines</u> for vegans.

Not that kind of survey Neville. Always make sure your research is relevant to the brief.

3) Carry out your research, then <u>summarise</u> what you've found on a page of your portfolio. You can then use this research to help you plan your dishes.

Part 2 — The 'Technical Skill' Dishes

1) In this part, you'll need to plan and cook 3 or 4 dishes using the <u>information</u> you found in <u>Part 1</u>.

2) It's helpful to start by making a <u>mind map</u> of dishes that fit your task. You can narrow down your choices by making a list of <u>important things</u> your dish should <u>achieve</u>, such as:

- Do my dishes agree with my <u>task</u> and <u>research</u> findings?
- Am I capable of making the dish to a <u>high standard</u>?
- Does the dish show off enough <u>technical skills</u>? E.g. dough making, making a sauce.
- How much will the dish <u>cost</u> to make, and will I be able to <u>find</u> the ingredients?
- Does the dish follow <u>nutritional guidelines</u>?

3) When you've chosen your dishes, write a <u>brief summary</u> of the <u>technical skills</u> required for each.

4) You should <u>avoid</u> using ready-prepared ingredients in this task — preparing "fiddly" ingredients yourself (e.g. making pasta, preparing meat / fish off the bone) is a great way to show <u>technical skill</u>.

5) Make sure you take plenty of <u>photographs</u> whilst you're making the dishes (especially when carrying out technical skills) — you'll need to put these in your portfolio / report to <u>prove</u> what you've done.

You should work hygienically and safely when cooking, or you'll lose marks (or a finger).

6) You will need to add information about these dishes to your portfolio. There are lots of ways you can structure this information, but remember to talk about <u>why</u> you chose each dish, the <u>skills</u> you're using for each dish, and a list of <u>ingredients</u> — don't forget to pop in those <u>photographs</u> you took too.

Non-Exam Assessment Advice

Part 3 — Planning and Making the Final Dishes

1) Next, you'll have to make three final dishes. These should relate to the task, and benefit from your <u>research</u> and <u>technical dishes</u>, but they <u>cannot</u> be the same as your technical dishes.

You could make three main courses, or you could make a starter, main and dessert.

2) E.g. if your technical dish was a vegan pasta bake with homemade pasta, your final dish could be a vegan ravioli with homemade pasta and sauce.

3) Give a <u>written explanation</u> for each dish you plan to make. Say how they fit the <u>task</u>, any <u>technical skills</u> you'll use, plus any further reasoning (e.g. if results of <u>sensory tests</u> led to any changes).

4) On the day, you'll have <u>three hours</u> to <u>prepare</u>, <u>cook</u> and <u>present</u> all three dishes, so you'll need a time plan to keep you on track.

5) Make a time plan that's easy to understand, and include timings, what you need to do at each stage, as well as any <u>food safety</u> notes.

Time	What I need to do	Notes / Health & Safety
9:00	Weigh out my flour, salt, cheese, spinach (etc) for my <u>ravioli dish</u>.	Wipe surfaces with antibacterial cleaner beforehand (and after handling any raw ingredients).
9:15	Start preparing the shortcrust pastry for my <u>apple pie</u> by rubbing the butter and the flour together.	Make sure to wash my hands after weighing out the ravioli ingredients.

6) You'll need to "<u>dovetail</u>" your three dishes to get them finished in the three hours you have — this means that rather than making each dish in order from start to finish, you'll have to keep working on <u>all three dishes</u> across the three hour period.

7) Be sure to take <u>photos</u> of your dishes, both <u>during the process</u> and as <u>finished dishes</u>.

You'll be Assessed on...

- Your use of technical skills and equipment.
- Your ability to follow food safety rules.
- Your use and understanding of ingredients.
- Your use of cooking times and different cooking methods.
- Your use of a good time plan and dovetailing.
- Your presentation and any finishing touches added to your dishes.
- The complexity of your three dishes.

Part 4 — Analysis and Evaluation of your Final Dishes

1) This is the last bit — hooray! You'll need to write up a <u>detailed analysis</u> of your final dishes.

2) Your analysis should include stuff like:

- A <u>sensory test</u> of the finished dishes.
- A <u>costing</u> of the recipes.
- A <u>nutritional analysis</u> of the finished dishes.
- Any <u>improvements</u> that could be made.

3) Here's a (<u>very brief</u>) example of how you could structure your analysis. Yours should include much more detail though — the more detail, explanation and description you add the better:

Analysis: Vegan ravioli with a spicy tomato sauce
I presented my ravioli with a spicy tomato sauce and sprigs of parsley. The technical skills I used were pasta making and making a sauce... (etc.)

Sensory Test:
Aroma scored most highly (33/40). This is likely due to the herbs and onions I added to my tomato sauce... (etc.)

Characteristic	Tester				
	A	B	C	D	Total
Flavour	8	8	7	9	32
Texture	6	7	8	8	29
Appearance	5	6	6	6	23
Aroma	9	8	9	7	33

However, appearance scored the lowest (23/40), so I should work on making the sauce look more attractive. For example, I could work on making it less lumpy... (etc.)

Cost: Cost of recipe = £3.90 Cost per portion (250 g) = £0.97
This recipe was very cheap to make. This is in part due to my decision to avoid using dairy and meat, which helped keep costs low... (etc.)

Ingredient	Amount	Cost (100g)	Recipe Cost	Portion Cost
Semolina	500 g	£0.20	£1.00	£0.25
Tomatoes	250 g	£0.26	£0.65	£0.16
1 onion	110 g	£0.17	£0.19	£0.05

Nutritional Value:
The dish was nutritionally well-balanced. It was low in saturated fats (only 6 g per portion) as it did not contain any butter. It also contained lots of fibre (3.4 g per portion). However, it could be improved by adding more protein... (etc.)

You should include a nutritional info table here (see p.17).

To get high marks, you need to analyse the nutritional value, costing and sensory test results in loads of detail.

4) That just leaves the <u>exam</u> to do. Phew...

Exam Advice

Here's What to Expect in the Exam

1) At the end of your GCSE Food Preparation and Nutrition course you'll have to sit an exam. It's worth 50% of your total mark.

2) The questions in the exam will test you on all areas of the course — you'll need to know everything in this book for the top marks.

3) The exam is worth 100 marks and is split into two sections:

Section A
- Consists of 20 multiple choice questions worth one mark each — each question has a correct answer and three incorrect answers.
- Only pick one answer — if you pick more than one you won't get the mark.
- 20 marks are available in total.

Section B
- Consists of 5 questions — these questions may have multiple parts.
- Questions will have different styles and lengths — extended response questions are worth the most marks.
- 80 marks are available in total.

4) The exam is 1 hour and 45 minutes long — you should aim for at least a mark per minute, which will give you some time left over to check your answers at the end.

Remember These Tips

1) Always read every question carefully.
Don't write an essay about vitamin C if it's asking about vitamin D.

2) Write your answers clearly, using good grammar, spelling and punctuation.
If the examiner can't read your answer you won't get any marks, even if it's right.

3) Underline any key words in the question.
This helps you focus on the important parts that you want to write about.

4) Use the correct terminology.
Know your foody terms — GM, CHD, BMR... you can't talk about these if you don't know what they mean.

5) Don't panic.
If you really can't do a question, just leave it and move on to the next one. You can come back to it at the end.

Understand the Command Words

Questions in Section B use command words — they are words that tell you how to answer the question. If you don't know what they mean, you might not answer the question properly.

State You should give a short answer or list — you don't need to explain why.

Define You should give a clear, precise meaning of the word or phrase.

Outline You should give a brief summary of a process.

Describe You should give a detailed description of something.

Explain You should give reasons to show why.

Discuss You should make a balanced argument covering a range of opinions.

Assess / Evaluate You should use evidence and your own knowledge to come to a conclusion.

Exam Advice

Plan Out Your Answer to Extended Response Questions

Extended response questions are longer questions worth 6 or more marks and with a scary number of dotted lines underneath... They often use command words like discuss, evaluate or assess (see prev pg).

- Your answer must be well-written (good spelling, grammar and punctuation) and well-structured.
- Before you start an extended response question, jot down the points you want to make and plan your answer to help structure it well and avoid repeating things.
- You might have to weigh up the advantages and disadvantages of something, or cover both sides of an argument then form your own opinion.
- Make absolutely sure you're answering the question and not just waffling on.

Here's an example:

Question 7 is about food preparation and safety.

Listeriosis is the name of the illness caused by eating food contaminated by listeria bacteria.

7.1   Discuss the methods that both consumers and food manufacturers can use to control the spread of listeriosis.

[6 marks]

Consumers should follow safety and hygiene procedures when preparing,

cooking and serving food to stop the cross-contamination of listeria.

For example, consumers should wash their hands and equipment thoroughly, sanitise

worktop surfaces and use colour-coded chopping boards for different food groups.

Accurate temperature control is necessary too — high risk foods that can promote

listeria growth (e.g. soft cheese and pâté) should be covered and refrigerated below

5 °C in domestic fridges. Food should be cooked to the correct temperature

and a temperature probe should be used to check that the food is at least 75 °C

so any listeria that may have contaminated the food are destroyed.

Manufacturers of milk and dairy products can pasteurise milk by heating it to

72 °C for 15 seconds to destroy any listeria that might be present.

Finally, it is vital that food manufacturers follow proper food regulations and

have 'use by' dates, where appropriate, on their products — this is a

safety warning for consumers for when the product may be unsafe to eat

(e.g. because listeria has been given enough time to multiply to dangerous levels).

Underline key words in the question — your answer should discuss both of these groups.

You'll need a well-structured answer showing detailed knowledge to get all 6 marks.

The number of lines gives you a good guide to how long your answer should be.

Shows good application of temperature control.

Correct terminology with explanation.

This answer has good grammar, spelling and punctuation.

This shows good knowledge of current food safety practices.

This question is about listeria — make sure you refer to it and not other types of bacteria.

Answers

A note about answers and marks
The answers and mark schemes given here should be used mainly for guidance, as there may be many different correct answers to each question — don't panic if your answers are a bit different.

Section One — Food, Nutrition and Health

Pages 1-2 — Proteins

Q1 Low biological value proteins are missing one or more of the essential amino acids we need *[1 mark]*. High biological value proteins contain all of the essential amino acids that we need *[1 mark]*.

Pages 3-4 — Fats

Q1 E.g. bacon *[1 mark]* and butter *[1 mark]*.

Q2 E.g. Fat-soluble vitamins can't be absorbed by the body which can lead to a vitamin deficiency *[1 mark]*. It can lead to weight loss (especially if there is also a lack of carbohydrate) *[1 mark]*.

Pages 5-6 — Carbohydrates

Q1 Complex carbohydrates *[1 mark]* (such as starch).

Q2 E.g. obesity *[1 mark]*.

Page 7 — Vitamins — Fat-Soluble

Q1 Vitamin K is used by the body to clot blood and heal wounds *[1 mark]*. It's also important for the immune system and our bones *[1 mark]*.

Page 8 — Vitamins — Water-Soluble

Q1 E.g. citrus fruit (e.g. oranges).
Scurvy is a deficiency of vitamin C — citrus fruit, green veg and potatoes are rich in it, so will all do the job.

Page 9 — Minerals and Trace Elements

Q1 Fluoride hardens tooth enamel *[1 mark]* and helps prevent tooth decay *[1 mark]*.

Page 10 — Fibre and Water

Q1 E.g. from sweating *[1 mark]* and passing urine *[1 mark]*.

Page 11 — Healthy Eating Guidelines

Q1 E.g. Peter meets the guidelines of the Eatwell Guide by eating lots of starchy carbohydrates (e.g. wholemeal toast, bread and rice) *[1 mark]*. He doesn't eat any fruit and vegetables — it is recommended to eat 5 portions of these a day *[1 mark]*. There are too many sugary and fatty foods, like jam, crisps and chocolate *[1 mark]*.
You could have also discussed his dairy intake — e.g. the cheese and yoghurt.

Q2 E.g. a fruit salad *[1 mark]*.

Pages 12-13 — Nutritional Needs of Different Age Groups

Q1 a) Children need calcium for healthy teeth and bone development *[1 mark]*.

b) Protein helps tissue growth and repair, which is important for teenagers who have rapid growth spurts *[1 mark]*.

c) Folic acid reduces the chance of birth defects in babies *[1 mark]*.

d) Elderly adults need vitamin B12 to help keep the brain healthy / prevent memory loss *[1 mark]*.

Pages 14-15 — Diet-Related Health Problems

Q1 a) E.g. The likelihood of becoming obese can be reduced by doing regular exercise *[1 mark]* and eating less saturated fats and sugar *[1 mark]*.
You could also have said to make sure you don't consume more than the recommended daily calories.

b) Maintaining a healthy weight will reduce the risk of high blood pressure, which can cause CHD *[1 mark]*. Smoking damages the cardiovascular system — smoking less (or not at all) will reduce the risk of CHD *[1 mark]*.

Page 16 — Energy Needs

Q1 Men usually have a greater BMR than women because they generally have more muscle mass *[1 mark]* and a larger / heavier body *[1 mark]*.

Q2 An obese person has a higher body weight than someone of healthy weight *[1 mark]* — this extra weight requires more energy and a higher BMR *[1 mark]*.

Q3 $2000 \times 1.5 = 3000$ kcal *[1 mark]*.

Pages 17-18 — Nutritional Analysis

Q1 Fat: $30 \times 9 = 270$ kcal
Protein: $15 \times 4 = 60$ kcal
Carbohydrates: $30 \times 4 = 120$ kcal
Total: $270 + 60 + 120$ *[1 mark]*
$= 450$ kcal *[1 mark]*.

Q2 E.g. You could use vegetable oils lower in saturated fats, e.g. rapeseed, to fry with *[1 mark]*, leave the skins on the potatoes to increase the fibre *[1 mark]*, and reduce the salt and sugar content by using herbs and spices instead of salt or sugary condiments *[1 mark]*.

Pages 19-20 — Planning Meals for Different Groups

Q1 a) E.g. Use soya milk in the mashed potato rather than normal milk *[1 mark]*.

b) E.g. Swap the chicken for a replacement, e.g. Quorn™ or mushrooms *[1 mark]*.

c) E.g. The crumble could be made with gluten-free flour / oats *[1 mark]*.

Answers

Section Two — Food Science

Page 22 — Why Food is Cooked

Q1 Raw chicken can contain harmful bacteria *[1 mark]*. Cooking chicken at a high temperature destroys these bacteria and makes the chicken safe to eat *[1 mark]*.

Page 23 — Heat Transfer

Q1 Water is brought to the boil by conduction *[1 mark]* as particles in the pan vibrate and pass their heat energy on to the particles in the water *[1 mark]*, and by convection *[1 mark]* as convection currents in the water circulate warmer water around the pan until all the water in the pan is boiling *[1 mark]*.

Pages 24-25 — Cooking Methods — Water-Based and Fat-Based

Q1 E.g. You could braise the meat *[1 mark]*. This involves cooking the food slowly in a pot full of liquid and often herbs and vegetables *[1 mark]*. Braising is a gentle cooking method which helps to tenderise meat, making it a good method for tougher pieces of meat *[1 mark]*.

Q2 Steaming is healthier than other water-based methods *[1 mark]* because there's no direct contact between the food and the water *[1 mark]*. This means steamed foods keep more of their nutrients / texture / colour / taste *[1 mark]*.

Pages 26-27 — Cooking Methods — Dry Methods

Q1 E.g. Both roasting and baking use dry heat to cook food *[1 mark]*, but roasting is usually done at a higher temperature than baking *[1 mark]*.

You could also have said that fat is usually used with roasting but not baking, or that roasting browns food more than baking.

Q2 Grilling vegetables is healthier than roasting them because no fat is added *[1 mark]*.

Page 28 — Changing Properties — Proteins

Q1 The proteins in egg white denature when you fry an egg *[1 mark]*. The denatured protein molecules then join together and coagulate *[1 mark]*. Water becomes trapped between the protein molecules at this stage *[1 mark]*. This turns the egg white from a runny, clear liquid into a white solid *[1 mark]*.

Page 29 — Changing Proteins — Carbohydrates

Q1 Onions can develop a sweet taste when they're fried because the sugars inside the onion are broken down by the heat and caramelise *[1 mark]*. This turns the sugars into a brown, sweet-tasting liquid, giving the onions a sweeter taste *[1 mark]*.

Q2 Starch granules absorb water when they're heated *[1 mark]*, causing them to swell *[1 mark]*. Between 62 °C and 80 °C, the granules burst and the starch is released into the water *[1 mark]*.

You could also say that starch granules become softer when they are heated.

Pages 30-31 — Changing Properties — Fats and Oils

Q1 Shortcrust pastry doesn't rise when it's baked because the gluten molecules in the dough have been 'shortened' *[1 mark]*. Fat rubbed into the flour *[1 mark]* gives particles a waterproof coating *[1 mark]*. This stops gluten forming long strands *[1 mark]*, so the dough cannot become stretchy or rise *[1 mark]*.

You could have also mentioned the use of 'shortening' fat, which has no water and so there's no steam to raise the pastry.

Page 32 — Raising Agents

Q1 Any two from: folding / beating / whisking / sieving / creaming / rubbing in *[2 marks]*.

Q2 Bicarbonate of soda has an unpleasant alkaline taste *[1 mark]* that wouldn't be masked by the relatively plain taste of a sponge cake *[1 mark]*.

Section Three — Food Safety

Page 34 — Food Spoilage

Q1 a) Whole milk *[1 mark]* — bacteria need moisture for growth. There is more moisture in whole milk than powdered milk *[1 mark]*.

b) A pizza at room temperature *[1 mark]* — bacteria grow more quickly in warmer conditions *[1 mark]*.

Page 35 — Food Spoilage

Q1 E.g. There is mould growing on the tomato *[1 mark]*.

You can mention that the tomato smells off, that it looks different (cracked or wrinkly) or it tastes different / fermented.

Q2 Banana slices are exposed to the air, so enzymes will react with oxygen, causing browning *[1 mark]*. Lime juice is highly acidic *[1 mark]* — the change in pH will stop the activity of the enzymes and the banana slices won't brown *[1 mark]*.

Page 36 — Storing Food Safely

Q1 The food has not been stored correctly. The raw beef should be covered *[1 mark]* and stored on the bottom shelf of the fridge and the cake should be moved to a higher shelf *[1 mark]*.

Q2 The cooked beef is a high risk food *[1 mark]*. Refrigerating it will slow the growth of bacteria and extend its shelf life *[1 mark]*.

Page 37 — Storing Food Safely

Q1 E.g. dried pasta — *[1 mark]* it should be kept in a cool, dry place *[1 mark]* (like a cupboard) and in a sealed container *[1 mark]*.

There are tons of examples of ambient foods you could use, but the method of storing them is the same.

Q2 Raw poultry will have a 'use by' date on the packaging *[1 mark]*. This is because bacteria can multiply quickly in the food and make it unsafe, so this date is given as a safety warning to the customer *[1 mark]*.

Answers

Page 38 — Preparing Food Safely

Q1 a) Bacteria from raw meat or other high risk foods *[1 mark]* can contaminate other foods if they are prepared on the same chopping board that is not thoroughly washed *[1 mark]*.

b) Cats can carry bacteria in their fur / bodies *[1 mark]* and can contaminate food by eating it, walking over it or laying droppings on work surfaces *[1 mark]*.

Pests <u>include</u> pet animals such as cats.

Page 39 — Food Poisoning

Q1 E.g. The chef should cook the eggs to the correct temperature to destroy bacteria (above 75 °C) *[1 mark]*, use clean equipment to prevent cross-contamination *[1 mark]* and should follow personal hygiene procedures like washing hands etc. *[1 mark]*.

Maybe you've put down that the chef could buy eggs from hens vaccinated against salmonella — that'd be good too.

Page 40 — Uses of Microorganisms

Q1 a) Yeast is a biological raising agent used in the production of baguettes *[1 mark]*. Yeast ferments the sugars in the bread dough, which produces carbon dioxide that causes the dough to rise *[1 mark]*.

b) Bacteria are used in the production of yoghurt (an ingredient of tzatziki) *[1 mark]*. Non-pathogenic bacteria are added to pasteurised milk *[1 mark]* — these ferment lactose (a sugar in the milk) to produce lactic acid, which thickens the milk and gives it a tangy taste *[1 mark]*.

Section Four — Food Choice

Pages 42-43 — Influences on Food Choice

Q1 E.g. People with low incomes will only be able to afford cheaper food options *[1 mark]*. This may lead to a poorer diet, as cheaper foods are often less healthy, e.g. highly processed, high in fat and sugar *[1 mark]*.

Q2 E.g. A person working long shifts may have less free time to exercise *[1 mark]*. Sedentary lifestyles burn far less calories than active lifestyles *[1 mark]*. People who are stressed may eat more comfort food, which is often high in fat or sugar *[1 mark]*.

Pages 44-45 — Cultural, Religious and Moral Food Choices

Q1 E.g. People may buy food with the FAIRTRADE mark *[1 mark]* as this means farmers are paid a fair wage for their products *[1 mark]*.

Q2 E.g. They may not eat pork, or any products made from pigs *[1 mark]*. They can only eat meat that is halal (slaughtered in the Islamic way) *[1 mark]*.

Pages 46-47 — Food Labelling

Q1 a) E.g. All ingredients must be listed to comply with EU law *[1 mark]*. People with certain dietary requirements can safely pick what to eat *[1 mark]*.

b) E.g. How to store the product, the product name, the weight or volume, cooking instructions *[2 marks]*.

There are other pieces of information you could have listed — see p46. Award 2 marks for 4 correct pieces of information, otherwise 1 mark for 2 or 3 correct pieces of information.

Q2 E.g. Traffic-light labelling to give guidance on the level of fat, salt and sugar *[1 mark]*, whether a product is suitable for a certain group such as coeliacs *[1 mark]*.

Page 48 — Influences of Marketing

Q1 E.g. The product may be re-released with reduced sugar or salt *[1 mark]* or added vitamins *[1 mark]*.

Q2 Using film franchises helps manufacturers target certain age groups *[1 mark]* or persuade fans of a film to buy a product that they may not usually buy *[1 mark]*.

Pages 49-51 — British and International Cuisines

Q1 E.g. Glamorgan sausage — Wales — Cheese and leeks coated with breadcrumbs *[1 mark]*. Cornish pasty — England — Pastry containing beef, potato, swede and onions. *[1 mark]*, Haggis — Scotland — Lamb, suet, onion, oatmeal, spices and seasoning *[1 mark]*.

Q2 a) E.g. Japanese: Noodles, seafood (salmon, mackerel, squid), pickled vegetables, Wasabi paste *[2 marks]*

Award 2 marks for 4 ingredients, otherwise 1 mark for 2 or 3 correct ingredients.

b) E.g.
Sushi — Sticky rice, often topped or rolled with raw fish and seaweed *[1 mark]*.
Tempura — Seafoods, vegetables or meat coated with batter and deep-fried *[1 mark]*.
Ramen — Noodles in a soup, topped with vegetables, meat, eggs etc. *[1 mark]*.

Pages 52-53 — Sensory Testing

Q1 E.g.

	Tester Ratings			
Characteristic	A	B	C	D
Dryness				
Sweetness				
Saltiness				
Texture				

Your table should have:
Room for four testers *[1 mark]*
Two or more relevant characteristics *[1 mark]*

Answers

Q2 E.g. Testers should work on their own so they are not influenced by others *[1 mark]*, they should be allowed to drink water between samples to refresh the palate *[1 mark]*, and the tests should be carried out in similar rooms, with the same lighting, so that the food looks the same to each tester *[1 mark]*.

Section Five — Food Provenance

Page 55 — Grown Food

Q1 E.g. Pesticides are used to stop crops being eaten / to control weeds / to control fungus growth *[1 mark]*. Chemical fertilisers are used to replace lost nutrients in the soil *[1 mark]*. However, pesticides and fertilisers can harm wildlife / wash into rivers, polluting them *[1 mark]*.

Page 56 — Grown Food — GM Crops

Q1 E.g. To make it pest-resistant *[1 mark]* (or to improve its growth / make it ripen quicker / add nutrients).

Q2 E.g. Some people think that it isn't natural to alter the genes of crops *[1 mark]*. There may be negative health effects that we don't know about yet *[1 mark]*.

Page 57 — Reared Food

Q1 Free-range food is food produced from animals that are free to roam / live in natural conditions *[1 mark]*.

Q2 Free-range animals require more land to rear than factory-farmed animals *[1 mark]*. They take longer to grow / use up more energy than factory-farmed animals *[1 mark]*.

Page 58 — Caught Food

Q1 A sustainable fishing technique does not damage the environment or catch more fish than can be replaced *[1 mark]*. Bottom trawlers may catch unwanted animals in their nets *[1 mark]* and destroy corals and the seabed *[1 mark]*.

Page 59 — Waste Food and Packaging

Q1 E.g. Simon should be careful not to overcook or burn the meal *[1 mark]*, should cook the correct portion sizes *[1 mark]* and should store any leftovers in the freezer *[1 mark]*.

Q2 Cooked ham is a high risk food and can't be stored for long *[1 mark]*, so the offer encourages customers to buy more than they would be able to use or store *[1 mark]*.

Page 60 — Waste Food and Packaging

Q1 E.g. Manufacturing packaging uses up energy and non-renewable resources *[1 mark]*. Lots of packaging isn't recycled and ends up in landfill *[1 mark]*. Transporting foods with excess packaging uses more energy — this means more greenhouse gases are produced *[1 mark]*.

Page 61 — Food Miles and Carbon Footprint

Q1 E.g. 'Pick your own' strawberries might be fresher / tastier / more nutritious *[1 mark]* and cheaper *[1 mark]* than those from a supermarket. Strawberries picked at a local farm will be better for the environment as they'll have fewer food miles *[1 mark]*.

Q2 a) E.g. banana milkshake *[1 mark]*
b) E.g. Bananas have to be imported from tropical countries *[1 mark]*. Lots of energy is used to pasteurise and refrigerate milk *[1 mark]*.

Obviously, there are many possible answers here — I just happened to be craving a banana milkshake at the time.

Page 62 — Global Food Production

Q1 E.g. Higher sea levels could flood low-lying farmland *[1 mark]*.

Page 63 — Global Food Production

Q1 The UK has a suitable climate to grow a variety of crops / can afford to import foods *[1 mark]*. Sienna has a high income, so can afford to buy good quality food *[1 mark]*, so Sienna will have food security *[1 mark]*.

Pages 64-65 — Primary and Secondary Food Processing

Q1 E.g. Salting / freezing to preserve the fish *[1 mark]*. Gutting / cleaning *[1 mark]*.

Q2 Secondary processing uses primary processed foods *[1 mark]*. Wheat flour, which is a product of primary processing *[1 mark]*, is combined with other ingredients (yeast, water...) to make a dough which is cooked to make bread *[1 mark]*.

Page 66 — Food Fortification and Modification

Q1 Soya milk doesn't contain as much of some of the useful nutrients *[1 mark]* that are found in cow's milk. Soya milk is fortified (e.g. calcium is added) so the nutritional content is similar to cow's milk *[1 mark]*.

Q2 Fortified foods already contain a great deal of added vitamins *[1 mark]*. Taking supplements as well could mean Gerardo is getting too much of certain vitamins, which could be dangerous *[1 mark]*.

Page 67 — Food Fortification and Modification

Q1 Colourings make the sweets more attractive and appealing for customers to eat *[1 mark]*.

Q2 E.g. A consumer may have an additive allergy *[1 mark]* or believe an additive-free lasagne is a healthier option *[1 mark]*. They may be concerned about the long-term health effects of artificial additives *[1 mark]*.

Glossary

5 a day	The Government recommends that everyone should eat at least five portions of different fruits or vegetables every day to promote good health.
additive	Something that's added to a food product to improve its properties.
aeration	When air is added to a mixture to help make it lighter, e.g. when making cakes.
allergy	An immune system response to a certain substance (an allergen), e.g. in fish, nuts and eggs.
alternative protein	A form of protein other than protein from meat which is suitable for vegetarians (e.g. tofu, TVP).
ambient food	A food that can be safely stored at room temperature.
amino acids	'Building blocks' of the body that make up proteins. Our bodies can make non-essential amino acids, but we have to get essential amino acids from foods.
anaemia	A condition where you have a reduced number of red blood cells, e.g. from iron deficiency.
antioxidant	A substance that protects our bodies from free radicals. Vitamins A, C and E are examples of antioxidants.
basal metabolic rate (BMR)	The minimum amount of energy needed to keep you alive each day.
basting	Putting the fat that has melted out of food back on top of the food while it's cooking.
'best before' date	A date mark on the packaging of lower-risk food (e.g. dried pasta) that tells you when the food is expected to deteriorate in quality.
biological value	A measure of the amount of essential amino acids a protein-based food contains.
blanching	A cooking process that involves plunging a food, e.g. fruit or vegetables, into boiling water before cooling them in cold / iced water (often used before freezing fruit and vegetables).
blended sauce	A sauce made from liquid and a paste of cornflour and water / milk.
braising	Slow-cooking food in a covered pot that also contains liquid, herbs and vegetables.
calorie	A measure of the amount of energy in food.
caramelisation	The browning of sugar and the change in its flavour when it's heated above a certain temperature.
carbon footprint	A measure of the impact something has on the environment, based on the harmful greenhouse gases produced.
climate change	A gradual change in climate patterns, e.g. due to global warming.
coagulation	When denatured proteins join together, changing the appearance and texture of food, e.g. when egg white turns solid.
coeliac disease	Where the digestive system is sensitive to gluten and can't digest it.
conduction	The transfer of heat energy through solids by the vibration of particles.
convection	The transfer of heat energy through gases or liquids by circulating currents.
coronary heart disease (CHD)	A disease caused by a build-up of fatty deposits in coronary arteries.
cross-contamination	Transferring potentially harmful bacteria (or other microorganisms) from one thing to another, e.g. from raw food to ready-to-eat food via work surfaces, equipment or your hands.
cuisine	A style of cooking representative of a certain country or region.

Glossary

danger zone	The range of temperatures (5 °C to 63 °C) in which bacteria multiply very quickly.
denaturation	When the chemical bonds holding proteins together break down, causing the protein to unravel.
dextrinisation	When starch molecules break down into dextrins after being exposed to dry heat.
diabetes	A disorder where blood glucose levels stay too high because the pancreas either can't produce enough insulin or the body resists it.
dietary reference values	Estimates of the amounts of nutrients people need in their diet.
dry frying	Cooking food in a pan without added fat or oil, sometimes called dry roasting.
Eatwell Guide	Government healthy eating guidelines in the form of a pie chart that shows how much or how little of each food group your diet should contain.
emulsifier	Something that's added to food to hold together ingredients that don't usually stay mixed, e.g. oil and water.
emulsion	A mixture of oily and watery liquids, e.g. mayonnaise.
enzymes	Biological catalysts that speed up chemical reactions.
factory-farmed	Produced by an intensive farming technique where reared animals have little room to move.
Fairtrade Foundation	A charity that partners with food suppliers to try and improve their working conditions and income.
fat-soluble vitamins	Vitamins A, D, E and K, found in fatty foods, that the body can store in fat tissue for future use.
fertiliser	Organic matter or chemicals that make soil fertile by supplying it with nutrients.
food miles	The distance a food product travels from where it's produced or grown to where it's sold.
food security	Having access at all times to enough nutritious food to stay healthy and active.
fortification	When extra nutrients are added to a food, e.g. in breakfast cereals.
free radicals	Dangerous chemicals that can cause cancer and heart disease.
free-range	Produced by a farming technique where reared animals have more space to move and live naturally.
garnish	A small addition to a dish that adds extra colour or flavour, e.g. a slice of lemon.
gelatinisation	When starch particles swell and burst, thickening a liquid.
gelation	The process where foods, e.g. custard, are set by chilling or freezing.
gluten	A protein found in wheat flours, that makes doughs elastic (stretchy).
glycaemic index	A number used to indicate the effect of a food on blood sugar levels.
genetically modified (GM) food	Food that's had its genes altered to give it useful characteristics, e.g. GM tomatoes that have a longer shelf life than normal.
halal	Slaughtered or prepared using a method that follows Islamic dietary laws.
heat transference	When heat energy moves from one place to another — by convection, conduction or radiation.
high risk food	A ready-to-eat food that, if not stored correctly, could grow harmful microorganisms.
infused oil	An oil that has absorbed the flavour of herbs left to soak in it.

Glossary

intensive farming	A farming method that produces <u>high yields</u> (production is often large-scale).
intolerance	An <u>inability</u> to eat a type of food without negative effects on the body.
julienne strips	Small, thin strips of vegetables.
jus	A thin sauce made from the juices from cooked meat.
kosher	Prepared food that follows the requirements of <u>Jewish dietary laws</u>.
lacto vegetarian	Someone who doesn't eat any meat, fish or eggs, but consumes milk and other dairy products.
lacto-ovo vegetarian	Someone who doesn't eat any meat or fish, but consumes milk, eggs and other animal products.
lactose intolerance	A digestive problem where the body <u>can't digest lactose</u> (milk sugars).
lecithin	A natural <u>emulsifier</u> found in egg yolks and soya beans.
macronutrient	A nutrient needed by our bodies in <u>large amounts</u>, e.g. fat, protein and carbohydrate.
marinate	To <u>soak</u> something in a mixture of things such as oil, wine, vinegar and herbs before cooking (to give it more flavour).
microfiltration	A process where milk passes through a fine membrane to separate the milk from souring bacteria.
micronutrient	A nutrient needed by our bodies in relatively <u>small amounts</u>, e.g. vitamins and minerals.
microorganism	A tiny living thing that includes <u>bacteria</u>, <u>moulds</u> and <u>yeasts</u>.
mineral	A <u>chemical element</u> that our bodies need in small amounts.
mould	A microorganism that can spoil food such as bread, cheese and fruit.
nutritional analysis	Working out the nutritional content of a food or recipe.
obesity	A condition where the body accumulates <u>too much fat</u>.
organic farming	A more natural method of farming, e.g. growing crops <u>without</u> artificial pesticides and fertilisers.
osteoporosis	A bone disease where bones weaken and become brittle.
pasteurisation	A process of heat treating food to destroy pathogenic bacteria. E.g. milk is pasteurised by heating it to around <u>72 °C for 15 seconds</u>.
pathogenic	Able to <u>produce disease</u>, e.g. some bacteria are pathogenic.
pesticide	A substance used to <u>kill pests</u> such as insects, weeds and fungi.
physical activity level (PAL)	A measure of how active you are / how much exercise you get.
plasticity	A property of fats that allows us to <u>spread</u> and manipulate them.
poaching	Cooking food in a pan of liquid below boiling point, e.g. poaching in a tasty sauce.
preservative	Something that's added to food to slow down the growth of bacteria and other microorganisms so that food lasts longer.
primary food processing	Changing <u>raw foods</u> to make them ready to eat or cook, or prepare them as ingredients for other food products.
protein complementation	<u>Combining</u> low biological value proteins to give enough of all the <u>essential amino acids</u> we need.

Glossary

radiation	The transfer of energy through waves of radiation (there's no direct contact).
raising agent	Something that releases bubbles of gas that expand when heated. Raising agents are used to make cake and dough mixtures rise.
Ramadan	A month in the Muslim year in which most Muslims are expected to fast from sunrise to sunset.
ready meal	A pre-cooked meal that's frozen or chilled — you just need to heat it up.
reduction	A process that thickens and makes flavours of liquids more intense by evaporating water.
rickets	A condition in children where bones are soft and weak.
roux	A sauce base made from plain flour and melted butter.
saturated fats	A group of fats that come mainly from animal sources and are solid or semi-solid at room temperatures.
seasonal foods	Foods that are only available at certain times of the year, e.g. British-grown asparagus is only available in May and June.
secondary food processing	Changing primary processed foods into other food products, e.g. flour into bread.
shelf life	The length of time a food can last without spoiling or losing its quality.
shortening	The effect of adding fat to a floury mixture, giving it a crumbly texture. Also the name of a fat with 100% fat content.
stabiliser	Something that's added to food to stop mixed ingredients from separating.
sterilisation	A heat treatment where raw milk is passed through a steam chamber at 110 °C for 10-30 minutes, killing all bacteria that are present.
sustainable	A sustainable process or material is one that can be used without causing permanent damage to the environment or using up finite resources.
temperature control	Controlling the temperature of food during preparation, cooking and storage, to slow the growth of microorganisms or kill them off.
temperature probe	A device used to measure the internal temperature of a food and check it is cooked all the way through.
trace element	A mineral, but one that is needed by the body in even smaller amounts.
ultra heat treatment (UHT)	A heat treatment where milk is heated to around 135 °C for 1-4 seconds and packed into sterile containers. Also called ultra-high temperature processing.
unsaturated fats	A group of fats that come mainly from vegetable sources and are usually liquid at room temperature.
'use by' date	A date mark on the packaging of food that is a safety warning about when the food is likely to be unsafe to eat, e.g. high risk foods.
vegan	Someone who doesn't eat any products derived from animals, e.g. meat, eggs and cheese.
vegetarian	Someone who chooses to not eat any meat.
vitamins	Organic compounds that are needed by the body in small quantities to keep us alive and healthy.
water-soluble vitamins	Vitamins that aren't stored in the body and are needed daily (B vitamins and vitamin C).
yeast	A microorganism that can spoil food (e.g. berries). Also, used as a raising agent in bread making.

Index

Index

Index

FNAR41